Tomislav Buljubašić
Developing Innovation

Tomislav Buljubašić

Developing Innovation

Innovation Management in IT Companies

DE GRUYTER

ISBN 978-3-11-065306-9
e-ISBN (PDF) 978-3-11-065444-8
e-ISBN (EPUB) 978-3-11-065462-2

Library of Congress Control Number: 2020934718

Bibliographic information published by the Deutsche Nationalbibliothek
The Deutsche Nationalbibliothek lists this publication in the Deutsche Nationalbibliografie;
detailed bibliographic data are available on the Internet at http://dnb.dnb.de.

Preface

It can be said that corporate innovation and innovation culture are constantly in the focus of the business world and that many articles and books are published every year on this topic. I started this book a long time ago and then I put it aside for some time, because of the huge number of editions coming out. At that time I simply could not see the uniqueness that I could bring. Then I thought of writing about exactly what I do: corporate innovation in IT companies and the result is in front of you.

Every new initiative in my organisation was a bucket of new knowledge, every new idea was different and every innovator has its approach, so this journey of managing innovation is full of challenges, but it also needed to be prepared on constantly learning. In almost 15 years of dealing with this topic, I started new programmes, innovation processes and challenges, different rewards systems, but I was also faced with different environments in the three companies where I worked. Two companies were huge (>100,000 employees) and the third was medium-sized; but, like the first two, it was a multinational IT company. Times of growth and times of slow-down, acquisitions and sell-outs, all affect innovation; it is better to say that innovation is one of the first aspects that is affected. Leaders, as an important part of the ecosystem, played a big part during the time; some were eager to make changes, but some had the feeling that innovation is for someone else's company or business unit. Managing innovation is a fight in long stages where you must be prepared to start from the bottom at any time. It was similar to writing this book: only after I got some encouragement about the topic did I continue with research and writing.

There are few books on the topic of IT and innovation. IT is assumed to be innovative by default and is thought to be much more engaged in the topic than other industries. Hence, it is strange that there are a really small number of books that cover this topic.

This book should encourage managers in big companies to ignite innovation, startup owners to formalise it, and entrepreneurs to start their idea and build upon it. On the other side, developers should be inspired to change the status quo in their environment and students should be encouraged to do that in the future.

If I ignite a spark in readers or put thoughts in the minds of some people, my task is complete. I hope that some of you enter "the zone" as I did while writing this book, mostly in my backyard, on nice summer afternoons with my Jack Russell terrier by my chair.

I hope you will enjoy reading as much as I enjoyed researching and writing this book. In the end, I hope that the book will be useful and inspiring.

https://doi.org/10.1515/9783110654448-202

How to read this book

Each topic could be read by itself; if there are connections with other topics, I noted that in the text.

In the first part of the book, I'm writing about the initiation of the innovation process:

- IT and innovation – the state of innovation among software development companies and how product managers perceive it. What is the effect of having different shapes of people in innovation initiatives?
- Igniting the innovation process – an example of creating an innovation process from scratch by raising innovation culture, tailored to an IT company with a view to the innovation strategy of the organisation.

The next part is about the current state of the industry and looks at innovation inside IT companies:

- The fourth industrial revolution will change companies from the inside – very soon, we will feel the effect of processing big data, using AI, machine learning, virtual reality, IoT, biotechnology, 3D printing, automation, autonomous transport or the widespread use of robots. Technology changes future occupations and many of the current ones will be obsolete. In parallel, it also changes the relations inside companies, ways of recruiting, but also ways of managing and evaluating employees.
- Innovators inside companies – in the world of continuous changes and new trends, it is important to have on your team, department or organisation, people who think differently and who approach to problems differently. Often, it is difficult to recognise innovative persons, as they are shy and tend to hide their ideas for fear of being copied.
- Life in the agile world – agile is so widespread and used in most IT companies, how innovation can coexist with this methodology? Are agile and innovation contrary to one another? Customer focus and product innovation should be part of agile team thinking, but they are often neglected in fulfilling everyday tasks and finishing sprints.

Then I focus on the innovation process and its methods:

- Development cycle, agile process, innovation process – a fast and short development cycle need ideas that produce quick results. This is not easy, and sometimes not achievable, but could be adapted to reflect the needs of the future. Methods of design thinking, lean startup, design sprint and startup corporation and how these methods reflect the IT environment and agile.
- Reward programme and effects of rewarding – example of a reward programme and its effects on the number and quality of ideas and different approach

towards improvements and innovations with findings from my research using different reward programmes inside the same company.
- Brainstorming as an ideation tool? Could brainstorming lead to new ideas and how? It certainly has to be adapted.
- Life after brainstorming – brainstorming is certainly not dead as a method. How can it still be used for adapted innovation challenges in a special environment where the traditional brainstorming approach is simply not working?
- From ideation to realisation – there are a dozen challenges facing the innovation process implementation in a software development environment that must be pointed out, ranging from "space to experimenting" to "funding".

Next is the more psychological part – about the inner state of innovators and external effects that inspire or complicate ideation:
- Introverts as the majority? Introverts are the majority in IT companies; that means no brainstorming (only adapted method), no design thinking (they hate post-its) but a careful and adapted approach can bring results.
- Inspire developers – developers are creative every day, but how to inspire them to look beyond code and think more broadly about product perspectives for the future of the market/company and reach their full creative potential?
- Environmental effects – regional environment and innovation. How to put your company in a bubble (own ecosystem) and not let external events affect you and your climate? A look at the effects that work environment and open offices have on innovation and organisational culture.

Methods to achieve results and their examples:
- Innovation challenges – quick and simple idea generation inside organisations with the guide and example of how to set it up.
- Improvements in the development environment – improvements are part of the development process, but often they are forgotten and not recognised. However, they can trigger bigger ideas and ignite innovation culture, so they must be approached as a valuable part of innovation activities, especially in IT companies.

Thoughts on the future and advice for success:
- Life after agile – what is the next step in the evolution of companies? Will agile will be enough in the future transformation of work scenarios?
- Every engineer needs a businessman – the world as we know it may be run by businesspeople, but it is definitely shaped by engineers. In corporations engineers become managers, but what happens in startups, where there is no time or budget for such education? Startups are driven by their first success – their first product – but can they survive the fall of it and create new successes?

- Startups – led by the vision of the founders, but later, with growth they often have to reinvent themselves.
- Be original – how to achieve uniqueness. Insights into the effect of copycats and the case of the stolen idea.
- Mechanisms of success – other activities that should support innovation other than top-down or bottom-up challenges like corporate incubators, acquisitions, joint ventures, skunk works or open innovation.

Another step in the method that brings results, with reflection on "dark times" in companies. At the end, a look at closely linked discipline to innovation management – technology management:

- 7 innovation method – My method for setting up innovation activities in the organisation, from igniting an innovation programme to the tasks after initial successes, with special attention to the role of innovation manager.
- Do nothing in dark times – Is it okay to stop innovation activities in times when the company is going down? Should it be part of the company's redefinition?
- Technology management – What role should technology management have inside the company and how it can add value to innovation? The role of experts inside the organisation and the need for trend hunting.
- The effect – The effect that innovation activities should have on the software company.

Further resources and analysis can be found on the website www.7innovation.net where you can find further explanation of 7innovation method described in this book.

There are many quotations and references; there are maybe places where I missed adding some references. Please be aware that this is not done on purpose, as some of my notes date many years back. So if someone finds their own words somewhere, please take it as praise, not that I wanted to steal something.

Contents

1 IT and Innovation

> Software innovation, like almost every other kind of innovation, requires the ability to collaborate and share ideas with other people, and to sit down and talk with customers and get their feedback and understand their needs.   –Bill Gates

Information technology has had a high growth rate for years and there is a reason for that: a constant flow of innovations in technology, but also in business processes, as growing competition on the market has made innovation a must for every organisation.

On the other side, the top skills missing among job applicants[1] in the current world are problem solving, critical thinking, innovation and creativity.

In the ever-changing world of IT, it is challenging to create and maintain innovation activities. With more than ten years of experience working in three different companies as an innovation manager, I will try to give a fresh perspective on innovation management in the IT environment and show examples from companies all over the world. A software development environment provides many possibilities for innovation, but also puts some constraints on innovation processes that can be bypassed, bringing success to the company and innovators.

Using the agile process in the area of software development with its short cycles, it is a challenge to create and maintain an innovation culture. With this in mind, the following questions are raised:

> How to bring innovation challenges closer to developers and use their experience and vision to create new projects? How to set up fast and clear focus topics or customer challenges oriented toward new business ideas? On the other hand, how to inspire developers about incremental, often small but useful and money-saving, improvements?

As I mentioned, I've been working in innovation management for more than a decade. In that time, I was involved in creating an innovation programme using a new reward system that successfully increased innovation results. The next big topic was the creation of specially tailored innovation activities for a customer-oriented software company. Product innovation was also part of my efforts, but I will come back to all these topics later. Now, let's see what place innovation has in IT companies.

The environment in a software company is much different than in other industries and most tools and activities, which are common in other industries, must be either adapted or totally neglected.

Let's start with people. Software engineers, developers, coders, or however you call them, are a bit different from "ordinary" people. They are in deep in thought, don't like disturbing meetings and they often have short-term milestones which

---

[1] This Is the Most In-Demand Skill of the Future, Ryan Jenkins, Inc. https://www.inc.com/ryan-jenkins/this-is-most-in-demand-skill-of-future.html?cid=sf01001.

https://doi.org/10.1515/9783110654448-001

makes them people who haven't got too much time to think "outside of the box". Hence, the shape of every innovation initiative has to be carefully adapted to this special environment.

Processes are also a bit different than in other industries. Planning is done differently, and the time to deliver the new product is shorter as all process stages are shorter.

Deadlines in the agile world are focused on a short-term pace instead of a long-term time cycle in a waterfall system or in other industries. These make life easier, but can prevent innovation as shorter cycles could mean less or no time for ideas.

Sometimes it looks like we are working in a zero-defect culture where no errors are expected, as we are concentrated on new incremental improvements, but innovations need a different error-tolerant environment to allow for breakthrough ideas.

In addition, the export of software is done differently. When a customer buys the software, it is not necessary to ship it with trucks, trains, ships or planes. The customer just needs access to the latest release versions and the user rights to download it. There is no direct contact with the customer, no physical stores or warehouses, just websites and servers.

What is very positive in this industry is that here the most common thing is change, which is really important for innovation. Software engineers are used to changing direction, projects, tasks and technologies; hence establishing innovation ecosystem should not be a too hard a job. Software engineers must educate themselves and constantly be ready for change. So, the future where there will be no more workers but only creatives is ideally shaped for today's IT workers.

In a time when it's not so difficult to launch a product, but it's extremely difficult to achieve success with it, product managers are key figures in starting and maintaining innovation activities.

The product manager's view

Now, let's look at what is important to software product managers, here is an insight from a survey of 40 product managers in a software company (done with a colleague, Denis Faivre). They were asked to indicate how important (or not) they consider several tools and techniques related to innovation and product management, and whether they would do more (or less) of them.

From the answers shown in Figure 1.1,[2] we can see that the activities seen as most important are *input from the front line, customer interviews, customer workshops*

---

2 Denis Faivre, Tomislav Buljubašić: Systematic innovation: making innovation part of standard processes, The ISPIM Innovation Conference – Celebrating Innovation: 500 Years Since daVinci, Florence, Italy on 16–19 June 2019.

Practice of innovation-related activities

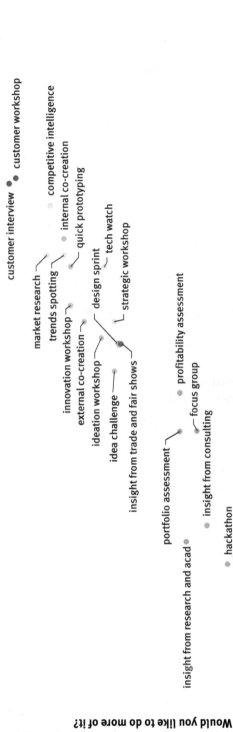

How important is it (for you)?

Would you like to do more of it?

Figure 1.1: Practice of innovation-related activities.

and *market watch*. We classify these as the most important practices in **customer and market intimacy** group (black dots), in which we also include *insight from fairs and trade shows*. Together, these are insights that make a direct connection with customers and the market as fast feedback on the company's activities.

Next come *competitive intelligence, tech watch, market research, trend spotting* and *strategic workshops* in **strategic insights** group (green dots). These are insights that could be taken from externals, but also from internal experts or strategic groups.

Quick prototyping, innovation workshops, ideation workshops, idea challenges, internal co-creation, external co-creation and *design sprint* make up the **innovation management tools** group (grey dots). This group is connected with the usual activities of an innovation manager.

The next group is less popular: *profitability assessment, portfolio assessment, insights from research and academia, focus group, hackathon* and *insights from consulting*. This is connected to internal and external tasks and connections.

Finally, we find *a smoke test* and *patent watch*, with a very low score: these practices seem to be not important to product managers who filled the survey. It would be interesting to investigate whether this results from a lack of knowledge, interest, or effectiveness.

However, this survey shows that product managers gave most trust to:
1. customer and market insights and research
2. technology and strategic insights
3. innovation management specific activities
4. external connections and internal focus groups

All four groups are directly related to innovation activities and are part of them in a larger or smaller way; and all are important in setting up the innovation ecosystem in any IT company. Product managers can change their thoughts after successful practices in organisation, but they will surely always state that the most important practice is a connection to the customer and market – so, this should be the most important aspect of every innovation activity.

However, the most important asset in this industry is people; but can people be grouped by some kind of creative perspectives?

People: I, T or X?

I first heard for "T-shaped" people when reading Tom Kelley's book *The Ten Faces of Innovation*[3] where he described them as:

---

[3] Tom Kelley: The Ten Faces of Innovation: Ideo's Strategies for Beating the Devil's Advocate and Driving Creativity Throughout Your Organization, Non Basic Stock Line (28 Nov. 2008).

They enjoyed a breadth of knowledge in many fields, but they also have depth in at least one area of expertise.

"T-shaped" people have skills with depth in many areas; the vertical bar in the "T" refers to expert knowledge which a person has in his or her "main" area, while horizontal means the ability to be open to thinking in other disciplines and to be open to using that knowledge. "T-shaped" people are great fellow workers, they will collaborate, communicate. In the IT sector, these people are ideal, as they have in-depth knowledge of their main tasks, but also the ability to understand the needs of other areas.

On the other hand, "I-shaped" people are mainly skilled in depth only in one direction, like a developer with expertise in one programming language, which is needed for her job. These people also fit into the IT world, but they would need to educate themselves because of the challenges of the future. Such people are passing the usual scans of recruiting and hiring processes, but later they could find it hard to adapt to future challenges.

"X-shaped" persons have leadership skills as they have subject knowledge of their subject and credibility, but also the skills to lead and support teams. Great managerial candidates.

"Tree-shaped" people have deep knowledge and experience in many areas. They have knowledge in the core area, but also a background in other fields, which makes them the best problem solvers.

In an innovation or creative process, these skills take their place and could fit several roles. It could be quickly noted inside of innovation teams which people have the skills to collaborate, think differently, the ability to lead or connect the dots and solve problems. It is very important to know people, but wouldn't this be too late? Maybe this should be done when people are hired. Many companies take care of various skills during employment, but many don't, as they just hire developers with the one currently needed skill, which will solve their current needs. Many companies are in constant need of a group of developers, which should be hired "now" and they don't care too much about all the skills people have; they certainly don't detect them.

It is said that to have a high IQ without social skills is the same as having the super-fast computer without an internet connection.

Therefore, "T-shaped" people can look at the task from another point of view, and as they have skills from other areas, they can be inspired and flown into the challenges for topics that are not their main area, a very interesting characteristic for future innovation tasks.

How to transfer people from I to T?

Job rotations or trainings could widen the perspective of people, but they must voluntarily step out of their comfort zone. They can make this step, but they need to be interested in other topics, reading and communicating to broaden their horizons.

IT-related	Creativity-related
I One skill: programming language / testing / integration/ ...	Expert Possible improvements
T One main skill and knowledge in other areas: programminglanguage and testing or integration and testing or ... + Communication	Expert + team player Possible improvements and innovations
X One or more skills + Communication + Leadership + Strategy	Expert + team player + leader Possible Innovator
Y Many skills: programming language and testing or integration and testing or ... + Problem solvers	Improvements for sure Possible innovator

Figure 1.2: Different shapes of people according to IT-related skills and creativity-related skills.

Figure 1.2 shows how different shapes relate to IT and creativity. "I-shaped" people could be experts in their field, but they would probably generate only improvements from their working field. "T-shaped" people with expertise across several topics have more of a chance of generating innovations than "I-shaped" people, as they have a wider perspective and more diverse knowledge. They are also a nice addition to any innovation team. With their leadership skills, "X-shaped" people could be candidates for managing innovation teams and have grounds to become intrapreneurs. In the end, "tree-shaped" people have the ability to solve problems with their deep knowledge and experience; they could fit anywhere in innovation activities. They must be recognised and be a part of the innovators community.

2 Igniting the Innovation Process

> Innovation has nothing to do with how many R & D dollars you have. When Apple came up
> with the Mac, IBM was spending at least 100 times more on R & D. It's not about money. It's
> about the people you have, how you're led, and how much you get it.   – Steve Jobs

Recently, I led a brainstorming session where 10 colleagues had 30 minutes to say one sentence about what innovation means in the company and to find a way to picture it. They coined the term "the fuel for the future" and proposed a picture of DeLorean, that famous automobile-based time travel vehicle from the film "Back to the Future" where the car is disappearing into the night. It was a simple task with a nice result: a team of software engineers made a smart definition of innovation activities and highlighted the future orientation of innovation.

In a recent study,[4] 85% of business professionals said innovation is very important in their environment, but 78% also said that their companies are focused on incremental changes. This is very common; executives are finding innovation as an important tool for the future success of companies, but it often remains only in words. Not enough effort is put into making innovation alive and then the whole process is turned only to improvements.

Igniting innovation is possible only in places where there exists knowledge about the past and future of the company, together with information about the people who make the company. Only by knowing the current state is it possible to make changes in the right direction.

Hierarchical systems embedded inside companies surely will not help with innovation, neither do examples of business units that are working as a small company without knowing or caring about other parts of their own organisation. Therefore, most companies need to start with changes to be prepared for innovation efforts.

As shown in the Figure 2.1, people, market and technology[5] are three things which are prerequisites for innovation.

- **People** – The right people are needed in an organisation, the ones that can adapt, learn and cope with future technologies.
- **Market** – Is there a market for new products, or must the company change the market or create a new one (there are cases when a very new market can be defined)?
- **Technology** – Do we handle the technology needed for new creations?

---

4 State of Innovation, CB Insights, https://www.cbinsights.com/research-state-of-innovation-report.

5 Tom and David Kelley: Creative Confidence: Unleashing the Creative Potential within Us All, HARPER COLLINS (21 May 2015).

https://doi.org/10.1515/9783110654448-002

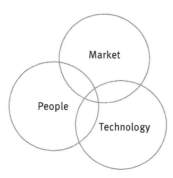

Figure 2.1: Innovation lies in the middle of the three circles.

The most common drivers of changes in the industry are new customer demands or behaviours, new technologies, new competitors and new competing products or services. Other less influential factors are economic factors, political factors and regulation.[6]

It is interesting to see what executives answered in one survey on what traits they wished leaders had more of to help their organisations navigate digital trends.[7] The most common answers were as follows:

- **Direction**: Providing vision and purpose (26%)
- **Innovation**: Creating the conditions for people to experiment (18%)
- **Execution**: Empowering people to think differently (13%)
- **Collaboration**: Getting people to collaborate across boundaries (12%)
- **Inspirational** leadership (10%)
- **Business judgment** (8%)
- **Building talent** (7%)
- **Influence** (1%)

It is easy to see that leaders are determined to include innovation efforts into their organisational practices.

Innovation culture

Innovation culture is an essential factor for good innovation results in any organisation. Building the innovation process, including the process of idea generation and innovation metrics, is nothing without a strong and active start of measures

6 sri innovation study 2019 https://www.sriexecutive.com/innovation/.
7 "Common Traits of the Best Digital Leaders" by Gerald C. Kane, MIT Sloan Management Review, July 2018 https://sloanreview.mit.edu/article/common-traits-of-the-best-digital-leaders/.

to establish an innovation culture, or in other words, an innovation climate in the organisation.

The biggest obstacle to innovation within a company is a climate or culture that does not support new ideas.

Innovative climate, innovative spirit or innovative culture – however you call it – is impossible without the support of the leadership in the company, which has to stand behind claims of innovation strategy, which should be implemented. The task of creating an innovative climate and culture in the organisation, which will encourage staff creativity and bring new innovations that will help the company, surely belongs to management. It is necessary to define the goals of innovation, both short-term and long-term, and then determine drivers for these goals (deciding on an innovation manager, innovation metrics) and an annual budget that will be available for the innovation programme. The budget should be available to reward ideas and to implement tools that will help with registration and processing of ideas. The new innovation strategy should be well advertised within the company, which is best achieved by pointing out examples of successful ideas when they occur. The scheme of incentives should be built in parallel. Everyone should know about the incentives after the application of an idea and the eventual success of the idea.

In the past, there was a time when idea proposals were collected in box for suggestions, etc. Today, this is often replaced in a way that proposals of ideas are easily submitted via a website (intranet) or a software ideation tool.

One of the most important factors is confidence in the organisation, because if employees do not believe in their company, they will not try to innovate. Also, let's state that a positive aspect that can affect the innovative climate may be a natural environment, like the arrangement of the workplace. Colour, light and space in the office certainly have an impact on creativity.

Let's define the key terms. Creativity is the ability and vision to do things in new or different ways, and the ability to create new ideas. The idea as a result of creativity must, however, have an economic value to be considered an innovation. Creativity at its exit has ideas, which may – but need not be – innovations. The first phase of raising the innovation climate, therefore, is raising the climate that will allow for creativity, and then defining the innovation process that will support the idea from the idea-generation phase to realisation. We can say that innovations depend on creativity, but creativity is only the beginning of the road that innovation must pass over in order to become a product. You may or may not have creativity in your business, but innovation will only appear if you have a defined innovation process.

When we understand that people are by nature innovative, but companies often are not, and hinder or stifle their creativity, we come to the challenge of enabling innovation, which is only possible by defining the obstacles that prevent it and creating conditions in which creativity can come alive. Individuals who have a proven ability to be innovative will find it difficult or impossible to be innovative if they are put in the organisation that does not foster creativity.

Innovation starts from the top of each company, which is expressed with the overall attitude of management towards innovation – innovation requires open support! The key is to create models that will describe the innovation process and support the generation of ideas in the company. In case of failure, there shouldn't be any kind of penalty, because it will kill the innovation spirit and ruin future prospects.

The biggest risk associated with innovation is not to innovate. If a company does not have innovation, it allows the competition to shape the future, and along with that, shape the market which will no longer be interested in old products. Because of this, we can say that sometimes the challenges of innovation are big, but the risk of non-innovating is much bigger.

It is easy to perceive that companies are always talking about innovation and that they love to fill their media releases with it. However, the same should be done within the organisation.

An innovative climate, or rather an innovative culture, can be achieved only if innovation is highly valued in the company. Innovation also must be a way of life and the spirit of innovation must be in all corners of the company.

People should have freedom for innovation and the task of creating an innovation climate lies precisely in creating a climate of freedom. You can't simply create a new process and tell people: be innovative!

Innovation does not occur with a single click, but needs inspiration, just like artwork.

It is difficult to know who among the innovators is just a dreamer and who is on the other hand, really focused on your market and on what your company needs – innovations for the end customer. Directors, therefore, have difficulties recognising true innovators who naturally need support in the realisation of their ideas. Big ideas do not always come as a bomb, but mostly as a series of small improvements and ideas that eventually grow to an innovative product, as a result of long-term work. This is only possible if the manager supports ideas that rely on one another with a common goal. Innovation is then drawn into the daily tasks of each employee.

Innovation climate doesn't equal innovation culture

A high level of innovation culture is naturally very good, but also a very important achievement to be proud of for any company. But the path to the right culture goes with the road called "innovation climate".

Tidd and Bessant, in *Managing Innovation*,[8] describe these two terms in the following way:

---

8 Joe Tidd, John R. Bessant: Managing Innovation: Integrating Technological, Market and Organizational Change, Wiley; 5 edition (July 10, 2013).

> Climate is defined as the recurring patterns of behaviour, attitudes and feelings that characterize life in the organization. [...] Culture refers to the deeper and more enduring values, norms and beliefs within the organization.

Innovation climate

The right ecosystem for innovation must be established inside the organisation; a few months are usually needed to set up the innovation process and build or buy the tools that will support it. The first step toward the right climate is the big support of management and the readiness to include innovation in the company's mission and strategy. The next steps include internal marketing, the dedication of resources and starting with idea management.

Internal marketing must be done using the step-by-step introduction of a new innovation programme or process, it must reach everyone and everyone must know that ideas could come from each part of the company and from each employee. Methods for doing this could be intranet, posters, e-mails, newsletters, management letters or similar.

Idea management needs a process and a tool. The process must be built carefully and in keeping with the style of the organisation's history and environment. The tool should be simple and easy-to-use, but capable of extracting some statistics and upgradable for the next challenge after the initial setting up of the system.

Innovation culture

Innovation culture needs more time; it needs to get to everyone in the company and everyone has to be aware of innovation. But, when do we know that we have established an innovation culture? Of course, it could be measured by the number of ideas, the quality of ideas and the number of innovators, but true innovation culture must be felt.

Everyone can feel when the right wheels are turning, when ideas are coming in and they are smoothly processed or softly rejected. If people start to speak about ideas, then an innovation engine is in motion.

Shortly, the climate will shape the environment, but the culture will put it into life.

Here are some answers to the question of how to establish a climate of innovation:

- Fear must be removed from any organisation that wants to have a climate of innovation; no fear of submitting ideas must be allowed. In addition, there should be no fear of an idea being dropped, as every idea is welcome. Nothing bad can happen to any innovator, nobody will laugh at ideas and nobody will comment on ideas after rejection if it isn't necessary.
- Errors are possible and normal in the innovation process. This must be known to anyone who participates in an innovation programme.
- Raise brainstorming workshops to a higher level, preparing it and adapting it for special cases and environments.

Figure 2.2: Prerequisites for establishing an innovation culture.

- Establish an innovation process, if possible, supported by corresponding software tools that are aligned with the company's targets.
- New employees can be a source of innovation and should be included in the process using awareness workshops and later including them in initiatives.
- Set up innovation as a responsibility of all employees, instead of the commonly held view that innovation is a task for only a few people. The company should be open to everyone suggesting ideas.
- Select the specific goals that you want to achieve with innovations, but be careful that these goals will not fetter the initiative.

Inside the organisation, there must be an individual or team of people who are active in promoting, supporting and driving innovations. We can call them innovation managers, chief innovation officers, person responsible for innovation or similar.

The primary roles of local "heroes" or "idea champions" in the organisation
1. must be well-known within the organisation as innovative persons and open to all questions and suggestions
2. constantly manage and improve the innovation system
3. ensure that everyone knows the process of creating ideas – how to apply the idea?
4. care for the ideas that stay longer in the innovation system without estimation
5. know about each submission of an idea
6. manage innovation metrics: the number of reported ideas, the number of realised ideas and creating new innovation metrics if necessary

Other roles, such as connecting entrepreneurs inside and outside the organisation with the idea creator, can be – but are not always – part of the innovation system and can be driven by another person.

Now I will give my example of creating an innovation programme from scratch, tailored to an IT company.

Innovation programme

Before starting a new innovation programme in the company, the state of the innovation climate was not satisfactory. It can be said that the number of submitted ideas per year, and the number of successful ideas, were not of acceptable value despite the fact that the company had an innovation process in place.

The first task was to build up a new innovation portal that had all the information about submitting ideas and about the innovation process. Next, it was fully translated into the local language, even the legal text about patents was translated – the things colleagues understand the least.

An award programme was created and promoted with intranet news, posters and articles on an innovation portal. The idea was to give monetary awards to the 10 best idea submitters with the most successful ideas in one year.

The award budget was approved at the start of the fiscal year and awards were announced on the innovation portal. The current position of every innovator in the award programme was listed in a table and placed on the award programme intranet site.

Types of ideas
The three main pillars of innovation power inside the company were improvements, innovations and patents. They were simply defined:

Improvements are incremental ideas that generate savings in existing products or processes.

Innovations are new business ideas that can make a new profit. After submission, innovations were sent to experts from the corresponding sector, who make an analysis about their possible realisation based on the customer situation and state of the market.

Inventions were handled centrally in the company with the help of the country's patent office.

Results
Already after the first year of the award programme, we were fortunate to register a strong success. The number of filed and the number of successful ideas has grown seven times. Workshops in all locations and strongly informing employees about innovation activities, together with publishing success stories, made for quick results. Figure 2.3 shows that the number of submitted ideas grew in years 1 and 2

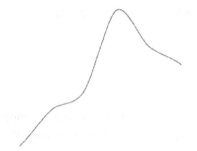

Year −1 Year 0 Year 1 Year 2 Year 3 Year 4

Figure 2.3: Number of submitted ideas.

(the first 2 years of the new innovation programme), but it is more significant to see growth in the number of successful ideas in Figure 2.4.

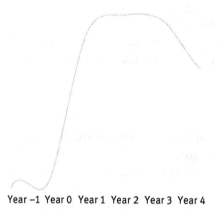

Year −1 Year 0 Year 1 Year 2 Year 3 Year 4

Figure 2.4: Number of successful ideas.

On the first chart it is easy to see the rapid growth in the year when the bonus programme was introduced (Year 1).

This growth was achieved by actively promoting improvements, innovations and patents. Improvement proposals were handled by the superiors of the submitters, and the superiors were notified in time when proposals had to be written by an idea submitter. A short discussion was usually enough to understand the proposal and decide about its future. A quick guide on how to evaluate improvements was available on the intranet and many superiors participated in a short training about it. This brought quick results.

Innovations were promoted in such a way that business ideas should have a strong relationship with a current business or with a current customer. The closer the submitter was to the customer, the bigger the opportunity to have a successful innovation.

The best innovators were recognised inside the company and were awarded in the bonus programme award ceremony, where they also briefly presented their ideas in front of management and other innovators. Abstracts of ideas were published on the intranet and in the award programme brochure.

This way of informing employees about successful ideas and continually publishing innovation news strongly influenced the establishment of an innovation climate. Other crucial factors are workshops held in all locations, where the innovation process and award programme were introduced, followed by brainstorming (idea generation) sessions.

Commitment from executives was the main driver in the innovation programme. We always had a strong commitment from the head of the company to the innovation programme and this was shown through the award ceremonies that were hosted by the CEO. These measures inspired known innovators inside the company, but also new ones, to submit their ideas to the innovation programme.

The award programme was alive for five consecutive years and the results showed that the innovation climate established in the first years was built on a strong foundation that also guaranteed a high number of ideas in the future. Later, when the innovation culture reached the desired level, there were new challenges. One was to make the innovation process faster and another to bring technology trends closer to submitters.

An innovative organisation not only has different processes, innovation measures, or leadership; it's the innovation culture that makes the difference.

Establishing and maintaining a high level of innovation culture should be the goal of each organisation that wants to call itself innovative.

Innovation ecosystem

Figure 2.5 describes six drivers of change in every ecosystem. Establishing an innovation culture is followed by innovation initiatives like innovation awareness workshops that evangelise this topic. Idea generation workshops should ignite ideation and calls for ideas act as the driver that should spark ideation across the whole company. The process must be supported and communicated through intranet or other means of internal communication inside the organisation. It is essential that the idea process is transparent and done in short cycles, but I will come back to this later. The same applies to rewarding innovation which will also have a special chapter later in this book.

Innovation culture	Communication
• Everyone can submit ideas • Everyone is encouraged to submit ideas	• Intranet • Technology trends • Strategy

Initiatives	Idea Process
• Innovation awareness workshops • Ideation workshops • Calls for ideas	• Transparency • Intranet tool • Short cycles

Support	Rewarding
• Innovation managers • Innovation process • Further reshapring of ideas	• Events • Company-wide awards • Special contests

Figure 2.5: First phase of building an innovation ecosystem.

Important factors for the success of the innovation process

Let's take a look at the most important factors for the success of the innovation process:
- set the end-to-end process
- simple submitting of ideas
- fast and transparent idea evaluation
- "gently" reject the idea
- "killed" ideas are later often reviewed because of possible new business opportunities
- the innovation process is measurable
- ideas are welcomed in the organisation
- innovators become "celebrities" and their success is propagated

Now, let's focus on software development companies. How many of these seven statements can really be done in their environments?

The first four statements are no problem at all. But the fifth? Is there a budget to look back to old ideas? Do we have time in this fast-changing business to look back at them? Often there is not, but this should be a task for the innovation manager who must regularly search his database of ideas and sometimes include old ideas to new challenges, or requests coming from the market or sales.

Measurable innovation process? Be careful what to measure and how to set targets.

The last statement is questionable in this environment. Do innovators want to become "celebrities"? We will come back to this question in the chapter "Introverts as the Majority".

Start

An innovation programme may be started with small, brief initiatives that will provide time to learn about the process and how it will best fit the company. It can start with minimal resources, and then scale up by learning about adoption in a company's own environment. If some new ideas are funded along the way and don't make it, only part of the resources should be spent. Sometimes the most critical thing is to kill the idea at the right time before it grows up without any prospects of a future. As the initiative will transform the environment, be ready for critiques, but also be ready to support evangelists of the initiative.

Corporate strategy

The times when big companies are not aware of possible disruptions are behind us. So companies certainly know that they need to innovate, but the question is how to set up an innovation ecosystem with connection to corporate strategy?

According to the article, "The Customer Connection: The Global Innovation 1000", by Barry Jaruzelski and Kevin Dehoff,[9] which includes data from 1,000 companies worldwide that are leaders in R&D, companies can be classified into three innovation categories according to **corporate strategy and understanding of the customer:**

1. **Need seekers** – invent the first product on the market (breakthrough product). Collecting information about customers and analysing their desires during the design of new products. They use existing technology, without developing new inventions.
2. **Market readers** – respond to what customers are buying – carefully watching the market – making careful entries with incremental changes.
3. **Technology drivers** – turn to internal research through technological capacities using breakthrough innovations and incremental changes. They observe and map emerging technologies and analyse trends.

A simplified look at the strategy could point to two different approaches:

A **play-to-win** strategy when companies take new projects to the market, aiming at open parts of the market using new technologies and new business directions.

A **play-not-to-lose** strategy when companies are focused on projects that will maintain the company's current position by following direct competition, and

---

9 The Customer Connection: The Global Innovation 1000 by Barry Jaruzelski and Kevin Dehoff – Resilience Report, strategy+business, Booz/Allen/Hamilton 12/10/2007.

without investigating new technologies or markets. The only advice to such companies is: *incremental innovation could kill you!*

A large company can't be a startup, with its products, processes, established sales streams and business models, but it can generate new growth by introducing new techniques like lean startup, mentioned later in the chapter "Development Cycle, Agile process, Innovation Process".

On the other hand, large companies – with their processes and structure that secure costs and improve products – are good at incremental ideas, but can't achieve breakthrough innovation[10] which is the target of so many strategies or corporate visions of the future.

It is important to have a company business strategy and innovation strategy in symbiosis. Some companies create innovation programmes, but they are not clear what to do with them or what should be the outcome of the programmes. When company strategy is not aligned with innovation strategy, innovation will not have much of a chance. An example is acquisitions and product strategy – a part of corporate strategy that is closely related to innovation strategy. Further, disruption of the core business must be an option for a company that would like to be innovative.

Future technologies that are just coming on the radar must be known and organisations must be ready to implement them when the time comes. Education and planning of resources for future hardware needs are all concerned with technology trends. Because of that, technology management should be considered part of a company-wide initiative together with innovation management.

Siemens, a global powerhouse focusing on the areas of electrification, automation and digitalisation has a clearly defined and easily understood innovation strategy:

> To be pioneers of our time and to work on innovations that matter: that is what we strive toward. Innovation means ideas with tangible benefits for all stakeholders. At Siemens, we draw on both internal and external expertise to develop solutions that set industry benchmarks. Applying a systematic innovation strategy is what continues to propel our businesses into the future.

Siemens also clearly states that everyone in the company can contribute their ideas:

> We invite every Siemens employee to remain open to new ideas; to learn to recognize the changes that are important for our customers and our own future; and to have the courage to implement the necessary changes without any ifs, ands or buts.
>
> – Siemens Innovation Strategy Website[11]

The company must define its vision, strategy and innovation strategy to know where it is heading. In other words, before you start driving, be sure you know where you want to go.

---

10 Tony Davila, Marc J. Epstein: Innovation Paradox Why Good Businesses Kill Breakthroughs and How They Can Change, Berrett-Koehler Publishers; 1 edition (June 30, 2014).
11 https://new.siemens.com/global/en/company/innovation/innovation-strategy.html.

I have been part of some strategy meetings that didn't produce any novelties. The reason was that company strategy was a blur and there was a lack of communication between stakeholders. The main assumption – connection with the market – was lacking, as market professionals were isolated with no connection with innovation activities. Also, a clear statement on how to proceed concerning product and market development was missing. Without everybody working toward a common goal and without a clear company strategy, innovation activities can be convicted to death before they even get started.

How much time and effort to spend on innovation activities? Let's take the example of Coca-Cola's marketing strategy where they invest 70% on the established and successful programme; 20% on new or emerging trends; and 10% on new non-tested ideas.[12]

Google has used 70-20-10 rule[13] for more than a decade. This rule teaches us that everyone in the company should spend:
-   70% of the time on the core business
-   20% of the time on projects related to current business
-   10% of the time on new businesses

These principles should set up new opportunities and strengthen product innovation efforts.

Some companies are dedicating time for innovation by their employees, as in widely-known examples like "Thinking Fridays" at IBM, or 15% of the time for ideas at 3M, or 20% of the time at Google.

An interesting example of a different approach towards company culture comes from Amazon, where company executives don't create PowerPoint presentations, but six-page essays to be read at the beginning of each meeting.[14]

Smaller vs. bigger companies

Strategy, the ability to change and innovation attitude change with the size of the company. Startups and smaller companies invest in their development and innovation as a need to stay alive on the market, but bigger companies more often turn to

---

12 Cris Beswick, Derek Bishop and Jo Geraghty: Building a Culture of Innovation, Kogan Page; 1 edition (3 Dec. 2015).

13 https://www.huffingtonpost.co.uk/danny-whatmough/bringing-702010-innovatio_b_1753246.html.

14 Aine Cain (Business Insider): At Amazon, Jeff Bezos has strict instructions for crafting the perfect memo – and he said it should take days to write.
  https://www.businessinsider.com/amazon-ceo-jeff-bezos-memo-advice-2018-4.

incremental ideas which are safer and which will create new value for their existing products.

Do small companies risk more? They are focused on product innovation and can more quickly pivot and realise new products than large companies can. On the other hand, larger companies can allow themselves to invest in more risky attempts at radical innovation, but they must build an ecosystem with a climate that will allow such attempts and avoid the usual traps like time-consuming processes or the ability to allocate needed resources from current products.

Edison's questions

Let's take a look at the example from one of the greatest innovators and inventors in history, Thomas Edison. In the book, *Innovate like Edison*,[15] authors Michael J. Gelb and Sarah Miller Caldicott describe the way in which Edison started his innovation efforts by asking himself the following questions: Which needs do people have that we can satisfy?

– What trend or trends are currently available?
– Which needs do they present?
– What are currents gaps in the market?
– How can I affect the ones I know of, in this category of industry, so that it makes sense for my lab and my brand?
– How can I test the usability of my idea?

Direct questions, asked more than a century ago, but still relevant and useful.

Types of companies according to technology adoption

When we put companies on a graph like the one below, where companies are compared according to technology adoption, it is easy to group them. It can be said that every company can quickly and easily put itself off on the curve.

First movers are all companies that invest in research, new inventions and breakthrough innovations. There are not many companies of this kind in any sector. They are leaders and they make trends. What is important is that these companies are able to make inventions.

15 Michael J. Gelb, Sarah Miller Caldicott: Innovate Like Edison: The Five-Step System for Breakthrough Business Success Plume; Reprint edition (October 28, 2008).

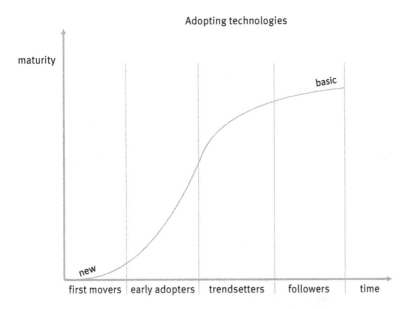

Figure 2.6: Companies compared by how they adopt technologies over time.

The number of companies is growing as we are going up on the curve. Most software companies are early adopters or trendsetters. These companies are still strong in innovation, as they have to keep up with the best.

Followers – at the end of the line – must do something to change their place or they will not be in charge of their own future.

Startups could be first movers and leaders in the new niche, but after some time their product will become part of standard technology and then (or, preferably, earlier) they have to reinvent/pivot/transform the company to be able to change the product or to place new product(s) on the market. If not, their numbers will begin to drop and the company will be in trouble.

High performers (first movers and early adopters) are five times more likely [16] to build a culture of innovation across every business function than low performers (followers).

The case of successful trendsetters

But what about when your company is a trendsetter or a follower and has no innovation activities, but still has remarkable results and is growing? Should it be changed? Should innovation be introduced if the company is doing really well without it?

---

[16] State of Innovation, CB Insights, https://www.cbinsights.com/research-state-of-innovation-report.

There are many companies that only react to customer wishes and market trends (also with respect to technology). They have positive results and are growing, but still don't have any kind of innovation process. They feel that the new features they are bringing to market are not innovative as they are the product of customer wishes. They certainly know that they are followers and their life is easier under the umbrella that they made for themselves.

But what if the innovation process is introduced? There are certainly many potential ideas in these organisations, but they are just not recognised. In addition, innovators in such companies don't feel comfortable and often quit, as they can't fulfil their inner call for the realisation of ideas. This can be changed by introducing a shaped innovation process, which will recognise every idea, starting with incremental ideas and improvements. This could be the start of company-wide change, which must be triggered from the top. Also, this will open up a new perspective as some colleagues will feel recognised, but also managers will see that they can enrich their products with extra strength coming from the inside. A transparent and short process should make things easy for idea submitters, but also anyone managing ideas. A way to introduce bigger changes in such an environment are calls for ideas described in the chapter "Innovation Challenges", which should establish the way that new ideas could come from the inside.

It is a big challenge for a company living in an agile process environment to make a way for new thoughts and inputs into the current process of user stories and sprints. Surely, the current agile process also needs evolution, which should add internal ideas to its short cycle. The question for such companies is: what could happen with the status quo? Is it dangerous for the prosperity of the company to disturb it?

Nevertheless, the change can positively reshape the company, which will then have loyal employees or a new group of innovators which wasn't recognised before.

Maybe this will not reinvent the company in a way that it becomes an early adopter (or trendsetter), but the positive effect of innovation will set a way for new ideas which could trigger such change.

Scanning

Before starting to think about an innovation initiative, the company must be scanned for its ability to implement any programmes. Interviews, surveys or meetings with human resources, strategy, product management, sales and the CEO will surely help in scanning the current state of the company. HR and strategy should be the nearest persons in the company to innovation managers and the CEO should certainly support this.

To scan the company it is necessary to ask the following questions:
- How is innovation aligned with strategy?

- Is there a project that should expand the current portfolio? Are they an exception or common thing?
- Does management support innovation initiatives? With resources?
- Are there rewards or a kind of incentive system?
- Improvements are tracked? Processes are constantly improved across the organisation?
- Are most people coached for innovation?
- Is innovation considered an important pillar of the organisation and supported by management?
- Are we able to take people from projects and add them to innovation projects in the future?

Toxic atmosphere

In toxic environments, the mindset is often determined by innovation-killing objections (not invented here, why change this, can we do it ...). In such an environment, people just do their work and don't care too much about it, or they don't want to hear of any activities above their work duties. Here, it is necessary to connect employees with the company and its vision. Scanning the organisational culture will uncover root problems, which must be removed to make innovation attempts possible and avoid "suicidal missions". Every employee should feel important with tasks, which contribute to the company's vision. Providing the right information, and giving everyone access to it, will be a step in the right direction as people with a wider vision and understanding of the strategy will be a step closer towards bringing everyone in line to achieve the company's mission. After raising the level of the organisational climate, innovation activities will have a chance and could be started. Still, there will always be some teams where the atmosphere is not the best.

There are also toxic persons who voice their negativity loudly so the atmosphere spreads to the surrounding environment. Individuals from such teams can still make their mark on innovation activities, if activities are accessible and promoted to everyone. Hence, from time to time company-wide challenges should be initiated to include everyone who wishes to participate.

Now, let's get back to raising innovation culture with an example of developing innovation awareness through innovation-friendly behaviours.

Example: Worldline – WIN awards

An example of a reward programme from Worldline – a multinational provider of transaction services with more than 10,000 employees.

The **WIN Awards** are Worldline's yearly innovation celebration contest. All company employees are invited to submit projects to which they contributed and which were implemented or significantly advanced during the previous year. A strong focus on the innovative character of the project is required. Projects are classified in four categories: client project, asset creation, transformation and small yet smart. After a quality check, submitted projects are presented to be voted on by all employees and the projects receiving the most votes are kept as finalists. Finally, an international jury designates one winner in each category by. The WIN Awards not only contribute to communication of Worldline's innovation achievements (over the years, nearly 1,000 projects were on-boarded), but also have a strong pedagogic role by stimulating thinking about what innovation is, how to characterize it and how to champion it.

3 The Fourth Industrial Revolution Will Change Companies From the Inside

> Whether we are based on carbon or on silicon makes no fundamental difference; we should each be treated with appropriate respect.   –Arthur C. Clarke

After the invention of the steam engine, it took years – in some parts of the world, even half a century or longer – to feel the effects of the first industrial revolution. Now, the fourth industrial revolution is coming much faster and the changes that it brings with it are revolutionary and (will be) visible around us.

Very soon we will feel the effects of processing big data, AI, machine learning, virtual reality, IoT, biotechnology, 3D printing, automation, autonomous transport or the different usage of robots.

Technology changes future occupations and means that many of the current ones will be obsolete. In parallel, it also changes the relationships inside companies, recruiting methods, and ways of managing and evaluating employees.

Will machines soon replace accountants, administrative workers, auditors, cashiers, but also financial analysts, general practitioners or lawyers? Could an algorithm soon replace legal services? Will professional drivers be replaced by self-driving trucks (at least on highways)? Cashiers in large stores have already been replaced in many stores. One word to remember: automation – all predictive jobs will be automated.

You may soon replace the visit to the general medical practitioner with a conversation with your cell phone or computer, where the app asks questions and analyses your condition with a camera and your smartwatch. At the end, it sends you to further searches or prescribes medicines in an automated pharmacy. Pharmacists are, as you may guess, another occupation that is threatened by machines because we already have "robotic pharmacies". Your smartwatch or cell phone will remind you when to take your medicine and its action will be monitored by the application. And the most desirable future occupations will be the ones that people do better than algorithms.

So which occupations will survive at all?

All "human" interactions are difficult to replace, e.g., process management, sales or human resources. Hairdressers, teachers, doctors, but also artists and creatives of all kinds, should not be afraid for their future. Employees in R & D, electrical engineering, robotics and software are already working on future jobs, but new professions are also emerging, such as data scientist, AI or machine learning specialists and innovation professionals.

https://doi.org/10.1515/9783110654448-003

In a report by the World Economic Forum (The Future of Jobs Report 2018[17]), creativity, analytical thinking, innovation, active learning, design technology, programming, emotional intelligence, critical thinking and analysis are marked as new skills that will affect business. The world will need more software engineers, HR specialists, recruiters, data analysts and business strategists, and fewer economists, translators, system administrators, journalists and retailers.

Lifelong learning and the ability to adapt and learn new skills will benefit a new labour market that will seek creators, computer engineers, health workers, and professionals of many kinds. Developers already know that their job is to learn new things. Without learning they will soon end up on the street.

> Many pedagogical experts argue that schools should switch to teaching "the four Cs" – critical thinking, communication, collaboration and creativity. —Yuval Noel Harari[18]

How will companies adapt?
Much of the change is already taking place today; digital transformation is also entering the last bastions of small and medium-sized enterprises that have resisted the wave of computerisation. However, some changes can already be seen inside companies as they are trying to attract employees, not only with higher incomes or promotions but also with better working conditions, working atmosphere, working space or events. An example of a major change in technology is seen in marketing – companies are advertising on Instagram or Facebook using direct marketing or influencers instead of 20th century marketing methods using TV or newspapers.

How will companies change their way of working?
One way is to use a model of a "startup corporation" with the ability to quickly modify and adapt business models and strategies, just as it is used in successful startups. In addition, companies can still use a wide range of employees' knowledge and built-in internal and external networks, as well as their long-term ability to perform, like rounding off the entire production cycle. In the new world, the winners will be the same as in history: those companies that innovated, those who adapted, and eventually those who copied. Many companies will have to change from within, by changing the culture within the organisation, and initiating internal entrepreneurship, creativity and openness to ideas.

---

17 World Economic Forum: The Future of Jobs Report 2018 https://www.weforum.org/reports/the-future-of-jobs-report-2018.
18 Yuval Noah Harari: 21 Lessons for the 21st Century, Spiegel & Grau; Reprint edition (August 20, 2019).

Radical changes – such as the absence of a hierarchy, the disappearance of working time and workplace, the disappearance or changing of the office as we know it – are hard to accept, but will all these changes eventually bring a system that will be more humane and more advanced?

Technology advancement should bring a better balance of work and rest, by increasing leisure time. On average, people are now working fewer hours than a hundred years ago, and the future should lead to a further reduction in working hours.

Many existing occupations will cease to exist, and people will be evaluated by their skills. That will change the way in which we educate ourselves, find a job or even how a job is done.

Technology creates new opportunities and changes the existing state. The only one thing we know for certain, the only constant we can count on is change.

> The new spring in AI is the most significant development in computing in my lifetime. Every month, there are stunning new applications and transformative new techniques. But such powerful tools also bring with them new questions and responsibilities. ―Sergey Brin[19]

Artificial intelligence

Interacting with artificial intelligence in the future is a challenge for companies, but also for the education system, which will be radically reshaped. The skills of future workers will be constantly developed. More jobs will be created, but what if new jobs are created[20] only where innovation is managed in the right way? The majority of the workforce will freelance and companies must be prepared for that with new processes for future workers.

In the end, the only workers that will be left to **work side-by-side with machines** will be the ones which can make product changes, as the future will bring with it cooperation with intelligent machines on a higher level than most can imagine. This is the foundation for a big jump in innovation for every company.

Chris Duffey, in his book *Superhuman Innovation*,[21] coins the term "computational creativity" to mean the way that AI can now up-level humanity to be even more creative.

---

19 https://www.theverge.com/2018/4/28/17295064/google-ai-threat-sergey-brin-founders-letter-technology-renaissance.

20 https://www.weforum.org/agenda/2017/12/predictions-for-freelance-work-education.

21 Chris Duffey: Superhuman Innovation – Transforming Business with Artificial Intelligence, Kogan Page; 1 edition (March 28, 2019).

One report[22] noted that fourth industrial revolution disruptions are advancing 10 times faster and at 300 times the scale of the first industrial revolution. Another report[23] suggests that the primary focus of innovation for industrial manufacturers are the Internet of Things (IoT), robotics and automation, and the Interface of Things (augmented reality [AR] or virtual reality [VR]).

Billions of IoT devices around us generate data and need some kind of control. The need for software workers and their innovations is rising and it won't stop anytime soon. To sum this up, let's take, for example, washing machines. Manufacturers of washing machines have had a stable process for decades; of course, it has constantly been improved, but there weren't any big disruptions. Now, almost every new washing machine comes with WiFi and new functions supported by the IoT revolution. This means that software engineers must be introduced to the parts of the industry that haven't needed such skills in the past. This also brings new innovation opportunities for all innovative companies.

In a recent survey,[24] 76% of executives expect cognitive technologies to transform their companies in the next three years. This will also change companies and all employees should be ready for the newest challenges. They will be retrained or, in the worst case, replaced. Also, internal processes must fit this change, and this will mean many processes and business-model innovations, which will come side-by-side with the changes in technology. Hence, software companies should invest in education in the newest technologies to raise the human capital of the organisation. In parallel, innovation and technology management must become an integral part of future companies.

Executives must be educated to know which challenges they will face in the near future and what investments will be needed. They should plan future scenarios and be careful with new investments, but also try to encourage continuous improvements, which must follow changes in technology. Many companies will face the challenge of building their own teams of workers skilled in AI algorithms; if they do not, they may soon face the challenge of looking for externals with such knowledge.

> Many people might share the fate not of nineteenth-century wagon drivers – who switched to driving taxis – but of nineteenth-century horses, who were increasingly pushed out of the job market altogether.
> —Yuval Noah Harari[25]

---

22 McKinsey Global Institute: The four global forces breaking all the trends, April 2015. https://www.mckinsey.com/business-functions/strategy-and-corporate-finance/our-insights/the-four-global-forces-breaking-all-the-trends.
23 Deloitte analysis of the USPTO filings data for the 2006–2018 period. From article: Pathways to faster innovation. Making bold moves in "the second half of the chessboard". Paul Wellener, Heather Ashton Manolian, Joe Zale. https://www2.deloitte.com/insights/us/en/topics/innovation/faster-innovation-patents-exponential-technologies.html.
24 *Deloitte State of Cognitive Survey, August 2017.*
25 Yuval Noah Harari: 21 Lessons for the 21st Century, Spiegel & Grau; Reprint edition (August 20, 2019).

AI is generating large amounts of data that need to be processed and managed, and companies that are first in finding ways to cope with these challenges will have an early adopter advantage.

Innovation management in the industry 4.0

The difference between a good idea and great idea lies in how human it is – and in an increasingly machine-dependent world, this is more important than ever.   *–Chris Duffey*[26]

Humans will be the centre of any activities in the future, our lives will be changed, but we will surely manage all aspects of this change. Some new disciplines will be created and innovation management will certainly change too. We will surely have more human-machine interactions, more data processing and easier ways to test, analyse and make prototypes.

In the need to provide solutions with new technologies, it is first necessary to formulate problems, which brings us to the same challenge that is facing innovation right now – to find the right people who will shape the challenge using market insights. As machines will do all the "dirty" work, humans will have a chance to focus on activities which add value. We can say that humans will have the best opportunity and the most time ever in human history – to be creative. Many smart people who are now coping with repetitive tasks or an unnecessary workload will have time to think about improvements, solutions and innovations; they will have time to be creative and their companies will have the possibility of affording "innovation time". This also refers to software developers, who will be replaced by machines in every possible task; but the workload will be even higher and the main skill that will be needed will be creativity.

This will open up many new questions and there will even be more talk about innovation, as companies will have to accelerate their innovation assignments. Here is just a glimpse of thoughts that will be open in the (near) future:

- Will we have open innovation for machines in the future?
- How will improvements be handled in work that is reimagined?
- Will the innovation challenges be started by artificial intelligence and will participants be selected by AI – as it could be efficient in finding hidden talents using internal data?
- Will AI manage the idea process?
- Could we make ultra-fast prototypes using AI and 3D printing?

We must leave these future challenges and get back to today's problems and their solutions. So, let's dive into the world of today's companies ...

---

26 Chris Duffey: Superhuman Innovation – Transforming Business with Artificial Intelligence, Kogan Page; 1 edition (March 28, 2019).

4 Life in the Agile World

Innovating is creating change. Being agile is adapting to change. The mindset is radically different.
$\qquad$ –Karine Sabatier[27]

My first look at the agile workplace was when I changed business units (BU) in the past. After working several years on a very successful product whose life was coming to the end – in the waterfall system, I started to work in a BU that was already working in agile. The first noticeable thing was that, instead of one dedicated project manager (PM) for every project (and dozens of PMs in the BU), the whole BU was working with a few PMs. The next thing was scrum meetings every morning for all teams ... Well, I didn't like that part much at the beginning ...

The agile approach is so widespread and common in software development that it can be said that it is used in the majority of IT companies.

Agile is a mindset and culture. During software development, the most important thing is the people and managing the teams that produce software; cooperation and communication are essential, and agile is primarily focused on that. It was developed with the intention to increase quality and speed. With less pressure on project management, it frees developers to work more efficiently.[28] Agile knows how to measure the productivity of developers, but does this prevent ideas from happening?

Let's take a look at a manifesto for agile software development[29] and its four main principles:
- individuals and interactions over processes and tools
- working software over comprehensive documentation
- customer collaboration over contract negotiation
- responding to change over following a plan

It is easy to read from this, that agile is trying to initiate communication, make things faster and be ready for change and customer wishes. This looks like fertile ground for innovation, but is it?

Agile requires its own mentality inside project management and it must be aligned with all internal processes. It is done in a small self-organising team with the aim of developing new value for customers. Many teams are working in the pseudo-agile process, not fully aligned to agile principles. Sometimes these processes are deliberately adapted because of the special environment, but sometimes they are just

---

27 Karine Sabatier: Being innovative and being agile are different, February 25th 2018.https://hackernoon.com/being-innovative-and-being-agile-are-different-1c5fef4db217.
28 Langdon Morris, Moses Ma, Po Chi Wu: Agile Innovation: The Revolutionary Approach to Accelerate Success, Inspire Engagement, and Ignite Creativity, John Wiley & Sons (7 Nov. 2014).
29 https://agilemanifesto.org/.

https://doi.org/10.1515/9783110654448-004

distorted with no reason over time. Then, the scrum masters should take control and make necessary changes if possible.

The next principles define main points around the agile world in a software development environment:

- Scrum is an agile process framework with three to nine members – who break their work into actions that are completed in sprints – working together.
- Kanban is used for visually tracking stories on a Kanban board, where various work items are placed in the right stage of the process.
- DevOps is a set of software development practices where people working in software development (Dev) and IT operations (Ops) collaborate closely together with a focus on the deployment of the developed software. Continuous improvement is encouraged in DevOps.
- The product manager acts as a product owner, and sometimes for some products gives the technical product manager technical responsibility, while the product owner stays more focused on external stakeholders.

The main benefit of agile is customer focus and the fact that software is released in a short time period with quick feedback. Every sprint (two to four weeks) adds new value.

The next benefit is constantly improving processes – with quick feedback, it is a must to make quick changes and all processes must be rapidly adapted. This also creates an environment that must constantly improve itself by learning or training.

Is innovation another benefit of agile? Teams should communicate and constantly try new ideas for better execution. This collaboration makes product development efficient, but is it really innovative?

Let's say that agile is developer-centric and process-centric, but it does not work in all environments. Now, let's look at an example of a strongly adapted agile product lifecycle process.

Product lifecycle process

This company adapted the process based on their needs and it has now existed in this form for years. The process starts when the product managers get input from partners (as shown in Figure 4.1), customers or as market insights and forward their ideas to the architects (part of R&D). These ideas are then roughly evaluated, shaped in a manner that fits their environment and sent back to the product managers who select and prioritise the ideas. They act as investors who must decide – based on the budget which features have priority – in a manner that could help sell the product. So, product managers have an essential role along the whole product lifecycle; they should coordinate and set the direction of the whole project.

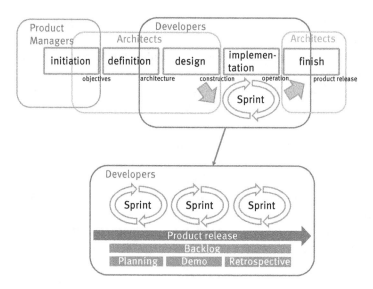

Figure 4.1: Product lifecycle.

Next, the architects could make broad descriptions of new features, which will be sent back to customers, but also to the development team who will develop them. So, after initiation, shaping of objectives and definition, there is time for architecture and design when the architects are writing user stories to the development team. When this task is finished, the developers could start with implementation in their sprint cycles following planning, demo and retrospective as parts of this process. After implementation and testing, the architects must confirm the developed features, and if all of the documentation is done, the new product release could be finished.

This, in short, is the product lifecycle, but where is the place for ideas if you are not a product manager? If there is no innovation process, then developers can't be heard; their ideas would only be incremental because they become involved too late in the process – in the implementation phase. Architects, too, can have problems supporting their ideas if the process is not set in a manner so as to be open to internal ideas, which are not coming from the market.

Are agile and innovation contrary to one another?

In both, the focus is on implementation, reality checks, a shift to self-organising and disciplined teams or optimisation – which have much in common indeed. These teams are ready for a quick change of pace or direction which is another great attribute of innovation. The focus is on a team that develops features and has a culture of delivering continuous improvements.

Innovation, similar to agile, focuses on the customer, but the difference is that innovation is creating change and agile is adapting to change.[30]

As commonly thought, agile should produce product innovation, but also process innovations as new ideas for process improvements should emerge in its iterative process. An essential point for innovation is freedom; if there is no freedom (time and resources) inside sprints, there will be no ideas. Continuous and strict time planning do not provide time for anything except working on user stories, so all innovation or improvement efforts must be done in advance, before planning releases and sprints inside the team.

The best advice is always to research current customers and then find new challenges and solutions for customers as a kind of design thinking method. Customers are sending companies their questions and wishes, but often don't tell very much. By answering customer wishes, organisations will only have new features, which could in the best case be incremental innovation, so the focus should be to hear the needs that customer is not mentioning. But how to gain such insights? In order to have radical innovations, companies must change their perspective and research. So, the question shouldn't be, how do we improve the product? The question is, how do we radically change the product? Or, can we step to the new ground?

In parallel to product development, a software platform must be added to track all ideas. The reward system must be established at this point, too. Retrospectives should be redesigned in order to implement first continuous improvements and later ideas that are more radical.

But, does agile –with its iterative and incremental development – prevent radical innovation, as there is simply no time or resources for incubation?

In my opinion, yes. The problem is that agile is focused on developing the next feature of the current product or even developing a new product, but which only builds incrementally on the existing one. Radical innovation needs time and space to grow and it can only be done in a parallel environment. Hence, any innovation programme must include initiatives that can motivate, educate and support anyone in the organisation to become an innovator. Education should give people the necessary entrepreneurial skills. This parallel programme must have strong support from above in order to "take" people from their projects. If ideas reach mature levels in the innovation process, innovators will need time to prepare prototypes, analyses and presentations; this is not compatible with everyday work as they will always be distracted. So, innovators must get some days off from their daily tasks in their development teams and be able to work alone or in innovation teams.

---

30 Being innovative and being agile are different, Karine Sabatier. https://hackernoon.com/being-innovative-and-being-agile-are-different-1c5fef4db217.

Can product managers steer innovation?

The product manager is the one who it responsible for innovation with the task of adding value to her product(s). Usually, it is done in an iterative way of continuous improvements, but this could also be achieved through innovation. In the end, a product manager can be the initiator of innovation activities (like innovation challenges). In addition, all of the project manager's external connections and knowledge about the market and trends could be a starting point of a successful innovation initiative. The next example could help in introducing innovations or improvements into the agile process.

Figure 4.2 gives an example of a complex Kanboard (as a tool to track the process, not as an effort to completely add the Kanban principle) for several development teams working on one product. The board is divided horizontally into swimlanes representing different kinds of tasks, and vertically by the current place of tasks in the development process. It is possible to include an "improvements" swimlane and place it below the features. Then it must be tracked like other tasks to get the necessary resources. When this is in line with the person responsible for innovation in the company and recognised as incremental ideas, it can help in raising awareness about innovation in an organisation. Alignment with product management should make the place of this addition stable on the Kanboard and add value to products.

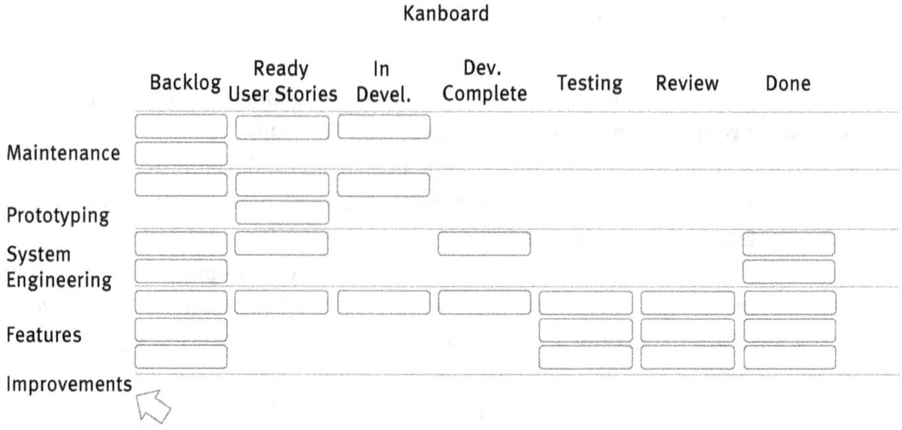

Figure 4.2: Kanboard.

Agile and innovation culture

The agile mindset in a company must be aligned with an innovation culture in order for both to co-exist. There can be a problem if agile workflows are stretched and the organisational culture is not the best. In that kind of environment, an innovation culture will be endangered.

Innovations, or even improvements, can't be expected in teams that are constantly "underwater". People working overtime will not have the time and energy for ideas, especially beyond their current work. The solution for this problem can come only from above – only the company executives are able to release some pressure to give space (even minimal) for fixing organisational culture and then slowly raise innovation culture. To do that, the strategy mindset of executives and project management of agile teams should be aligned.

The best solution for every culture to become alive is when people start to be aware of successful examples and best practices.

5 Innovators Inside Companies

We need constant change, technological innovation capability, and high productivity to survive in the fierce competitive environment.   –Joe Kaeser (CEO of Siemens AG)

In a world of continual changes and new trends, it is important to have on your team, department or organisation, people who think differently and approach problems in a different manner. Often, it's difficult to recognise innovative persons. They may be shy and hide their ideas for fear of being copied. Nevertheless, with time some of their characteristics will come along:
- Innovators have the need to fulfil their inner needs.
- Initiate new projects that will be guided by their ideas.
- Break the current status quo.
- Open new possibilities, visions and future scenarios.
- Innovators like to imagine and dream.
- They have a strong need to transform their visions into reality.

If recognised, they must be guided on how to continue and work on their creativity; initial advice could be:
- They must be ready for failure.
- They must be ready for critiques.
- They must find new paths for their ideas and have to learn how to do that inside the company.
- Always build upon the first idea.
- Be open to changes that will make their ideas better.

I had the opportunity to meet many innovators and they all have one common characteristic – they are curious, they always want change and they will never stop with one idea.

I must mention that innovators are often not innovative only inside their organisations, but also in all aspects of their lives. They will innovate at home, in the garden, on a construction site or on the playing field. And they will always have "special" ideas. If you ask yourself, you will surely find at least one innovator close to you, that you didn't ever connect with this word – maybe it will be more correct to call them "creatives".

True innovators are passionate when speaking about their ideas and they will do anything to make their ideas happen. Their passion can pull the project and the team along and make their idea happen, even after any other leader would have given up. It is enough to ask a person what is most exciting in what is she currently doing and all her passion will come to life.

https://doi.org/10.1515/9783110654448-005

Sometimes, we call innovators "rebels" who will not tolerate the current system in their environment. They break the status quo and should be supported in this mission as this could bring new ideas and improvements to their organisation.

It is clear that innovators are the key factor for innovation success. But, how to start a system which will nurture innovation?

Nurturing innovation

Setting the preconditions for great results

Have you heard a friend or a colleague making fun of her superiors because they are doing something "stupid"? Perhaps you asked, "Why don't you suggest a solution?" You might have heard an answer like: "They wouldn't listen" or, "They don't care for my thoughts" or, "Let them do what they want!" This occurs more often in other sectors, but I have heard examples of such conditions in IT companies, too.

This barrier between employees and the firm – let's call it "learned helplessness" – is the characteristic of organisations where employees quickly learn that there is no need for creative thinking or the exchange of ideas. This is a great example of a culture that must be changed. It is easy to see that there is no place for "bottom-up" ideas in such environments. In fact, ideas just don't have a fertile ground for realisation: *"This already exist!"/"We were this way for years!"/"Why should we change it?"/"This is not the way it works in the real world!"/"We don't have time for this!"* There are many excuses that maintain the status quo.

Some of the reasons why an innovator faces a wall in her corporation are often political (replacing someone who is incompetent), fear of change, envy ("These are not my ideas, so why should I support them?") or simple laziness ("Why learn new technologies when things could be done in an existing way?").

Political walls could be replaced by setting a bottom-up innovation ecosystem, which will allow everyone in the organisation to propose ideas. There wouldn't be any bosses to kill the idea in the first steps with some stupid reason.

Fear of change is ingrained in some individuals, but they would change their minds if the whole company, led by management, would embrace change.

Envy could be removed by putting all ideas in the same place, like an innovation tool visible to everyone. People must understand that ideas could help with work (process improvements), make the product more attractive (product improvement) or establish a new way for something completely new. Support must become a natural thing, as every idea will make the company better and more prosperous.

Laziness is the thing that needs no explanation. It is destructive and not acceptable. But on the other hand, let me just point out one thing – a kind of laziness could trigger ideas. Maybe it is not fair to call it laziness; a more proper description might be a desire for efficiency – developers don't like to do repetitive things and they will find the way to automatise. This is the way to create improvements.

Change is inevitable, but it comes in steps. After identifying existing barriers, the process of establishing an innovation culture in an organisation should be started. It will be an essential factor for spurring creativity in any organisation. The task of creating an innovative culture includes unleashing the creativity of colleagues, which will secure the future of the company.

Trust: The fuel of creativity

One of the most important factors in fuelling creativity in an organisation is trust. If employees don't trust their company, they will not innovate by sharing their ideas. The environment influences the creativity (the zero starting point of the innovation process) of the individual – or future innovator.

Creativity is, by definition, the ability to create new ideas, but ideas as a result of creativity must have economic value to be treated as an "innovation" inside a company. It can be said that innovation links directly to creativity, but creativity is only the start of the long journey that an idea must go through to become a product. We may or may not have creativity in our work, but innovation will only come as part of a defined process.

People are naturally creative, but companies often are not and are usually more likely to suppress creativity. Individuals who have the ability to create will not be able to express ideas in those organisations that do not encourage creativity.

The key to success is in the creation of models that describe the innovation process and allow the occurrence of failure – which is very common in projects. Indeed, the story of innovation is a story of failure, because only a fraction of ideas are ever realised. Some companies have a success ratio of 5%, some 10% and only improvements could reach success ratios of 50% as they could be born and realised inside the same team or business unit.

An innovation culture can be achieved only if innovation is highly valued within the company; it has to be a way of life and as such be present in all corners of the company. When innovation is the responsibility of every employee, we can talk of an "innovative company" that bases its development on the creativity of its most valuable resource, its people.

Key persons

There are several types of key persons in their relation to innovation. First, there are **inventors**; they are typically rare and if they exist, they must receive special attention and care inside the organisation to keep them happy and loyal. All inventions should be tracked and, if needed, the company must equip itself with an invention programme which includes special education and collaboration with the patent office. Next are **innovators**, people who use ideas in a way to turn them into a new product that is interesting for the market. They should think not only about ideas, but also about the commercial part of the process – how to place idea on the market. They very rarely do so, however, especially if special education and support inside the company are lacking. We can put inventors and innovators under the same roof as **creative persons**.

It is very important to have **entrepreneurs** who clear the path for these ideas and make innovators' lives easier. They don't have to be innovators, but are persons who know many in the company or can use influence to get resources. They may also have the skills of presenters and be a valuable part of the innovation team.

Innovation managers or chief innovation officers should establish and maintain an innovation ecosystem and be in contact with the **CEO** who must act as a driver and financier of the whole programme.

All these people must exist in an organisation to have an innovation engine in operation. In the software industry, this is even more pronounced. Creative persons are everywhere; they may only be active or inactive.

Innovation managers, or "local heroes", must be known throughout the organisation. It is good if they are innovative people who already have some ideas in the system and who still actively collaborate.

The chief innovation officer (CIO) in bigger companies (executive role) or innovation manager must have:
- support from the top. The CEO must have confidence and be generous with a budget at the start. Later, the link between CEO and innovation manager must not be broken and they must collaborate frequently, keeping an eye on their targeted values.
- the ability to develop metrics and track the innovation effects in the company. Metrics must fit the company's position in the market and the state of innovation culture without expecting a large result at the start.
- tools for managing ideas that will help in having a quick and transparent process without getting lost under the big number of ideas. Such tools must be managed and developed further to suit the company's special needs.
- the capability to provide educational training, such as workshops on innovation awareness, creativity, trend-spotting or customers.
- alignment with business units, which is essential in the early life of ideas, as ideas must be taken over by business units at some point. This means alignment with portfolio and strategy, but sometimes also an investment in new portfolio elements pushed by the innovation initiatives.
- involvement in technology management such as tech scouting, knowledge of technology trends and market analysis. The key here could be the establishment of some kind of expert network in the company.
- innovation skills and may even be a past innovator. She will then know the system from the inside (not necessary, but preferable). This will add the ability of an "insider's look".

- idea generation facilitation skills – there will always be a need for some kind of brainstorming session and the ability to keep a group of colleagues busy and entertained for an hour or two, or even a day or week, should be the part of skillset.
- the ability to take care of ideas that need special support. There are some ideas which need a special amount of care and time, and require a special budget, to be successful in the end. It is important to recognise such ideas. in contrast, some ideas don't need care and can be simply handed over to the unit that will realise them – in case that a budget is allocated and the market is interested. In that case, the person responsible for innovation should only track the process and gather information for a future success story.
- soft skills for listening to everyone with an idea in the company and with the skill to build an internal network of collaborators.
- the ability to drive company-wide initiatives with tens or hundreds of ideas.
- skills for gently killing ideas. Very important as people with rejected ideas have new ideas and should not be scared of letting them into the system. It is not enough to reject it with an automatically generated email; it is necessary to spend a few minutes and write the reason for the rejection and to thank the submitter. When this is done politely, people will not stop generating ideas after rejection.
- the ability to create an innovation strategy together with other stakeholders. Where are we headed?
- external connections or openness to collaboration with externals, including other companies, universities and startups.

How did I become an innovation manager?

When I started working, I was employed at a big multinational company where my role in the company was oriented toward software development. I had been working as a developer for a few months when we got a visit from a person with the title "innovation manager". I saw the two-hour company presentation with steps on how to submit ideas and with the introduction to the innovation process. It was short and I hadn't heard as much as I wanted, but I learned where to find further information. And really, all the necessary information was on the company's intranet. Soon, I submitted my first idea, quickly followed by second and third. Then I got answers. The first two were quickly rejected, but the third was approved. It was a process improvement.

Later, there was a company initiative on ideas and I was the one with the most ideas in my unit. So, I became responsible for innovation in my business unit. Now, I motivated others to be innovative and soon our BU had the most ideas in our entity. Two years later, I became the innovation manager for my part of the company and was offered the chance to create a full-scale innovation programme with rewards – a bonus programme.

I made progress by motivating myself and others to be innovative, something I'm still trying to do.

> Innovation is not just reserved for so-called creatives or leaders – it is for everyone. Those working on the frontlines, day to day, or dealing with the products or services, first-hand, are often best placed to make improvements and come up with solutions. –Richard Branson[31]

Innovation attitude

In regard to innovation attitude, people can be divided into three groups: those who create innovations, those who support innovations and those who "kill" innovations. The first are always open, positive and supportive to any kind of innovation initiative, they are the ones who should be part of the "innovators group". People from the second group – supporters, will support ideas, but will not get involved. The last ones are those who are hostile to new ideas. They are the ones who want to live without disturbing the status quo and they should be the minority in software companies. Often, the first group will not be the most numerous. We should take away criticism from "innovation killers", or convert it to constructive critique, and then move them to other groups. Similarly, supporters should be turned into innovators by presenting success stories and by slowly building an innovation culture in the organisation.

When igniting an innovation climate, any kind of announcement is helpful which can be done easily and efficiently internally. Posters on the walls, an intranet site, published interviews, videos, Instagram, Twitter or other social media, can make initiatives visible and attractive.

A kind of internal marketing is also the shape of the internal structure and the messages coming to the employees from the company hierarchies. The way the company handles internal processes could guide employees on what is allowed or what is promoted inside the organisation. Some companies put quality processes as their headline with "no failure" and "play-by-the-rules" politics, which then become common to everyone in the company.

I saw a company that had innovations and quality management together in one department: two disciplines with no common ground and almost completely opposite attitudes. One is driven by rules and certainty and the other is trying to break the rules and let go of certainty. So, many different and unrelated tasks and metrics were intertwined; in the end, this was managed as two separate departments inside one.

The next section describes an example of a successful innovation programme where the company was focused on their employees and gave them resources and a nice chance for the realisation of their ideas. Also, it had a way of including many people in a kind of innovation group.

---

31 https://www.virgin.com/richard-branson/i-innovation.

Example: Amdocs Shapers – first focus on people, then on ideas

Amdocs, a company with 25,000 employees providing software and services globally to leading communications and media companies, wanted to find a way to stay several steps ahead of consumer demands. How could they anticipate a new generation's way of consuming and interacting with content – not only right now, but in five years? So, they initiated the Shapers programme[32] to find answers to this and other questions related to exponential changes through disruptive thought and direct action.

The core Shapers team wanted to take a deeper look at the characteristics of ideators, which meant creating a multi-functional team of executives, HR leaders and innovation specialists. The application process involved a task-oriented, self-nomination process. First, it was necessary to write an essay about an idea, then create and send a one-minute video about why you are a Shaper, and finally the core-team would choose an initial 100 potential shapers. Afterward they would narrow the team down to 18 through a series of interviews conducted by the core team.

Over the next nine months, the 18 Shapers had done research and collaborated with internal Amdocs experts and outside specialists to grow their ideas into tangible outcomes. They presented their ideas to a committee of senior managers and external mentors and then validated their assumptions with end-users and customers. During this phase, the Shapers met three times face-to-face, for week-long workshops, boot camps, and idea-refining initiatives.

At the first meeting, the first two days consisted of bringing top industry leaders and talking on the potential uses of artificial intelligence, blockchain, robotics and other trends. Then, on days 3 and 4 they started the ideation process as complete 18 strangers.

Their boot camp goal was to find the five best ideas from the many ideas generated, using a combination of design thinking techniques, lean startup methodology and experimentation. Then the Shapers were back at their day job, but still doing research.

In the next session, the Shapers refined their ideas using the hothousing methodology, where a group of people meets in a room to work intensely together on a project for a longer period.

The extended group with a mix of experts in marketing, finance, strategy, UI, and external devil's advocates – the red team (dressed appropriately in red) – questioned any ideas that seemed superficial or narrow.

The intention was to test the ideas to determine which ones had a chance. The Shapers had the chance to choose experts and startups they specifically needed at

---

32 Amdocs Shapers: Bringing Breakthrough Ideas To Life, Tayla Landau. https://innov8rs.co/news/amdocs-shapers-bringing-breakthrough-ideas-to-life/.

their side in order to rebuild and improve their ideas. At the end of week two, five teams were formed, each with an idea to pitch to five potential executive sponsors.

Prior to the next phase, the Shapers needed to perform competitor analyses to assess product-market fit. Senior venture capitalist (external) mentors met every couple of weeks with the Shapers and helped them not only to refine their ideas, but also to make sure they were complete. This validation process ended with a presentation to the CEO as part of Innovation Week, after which four winning ideas would be selected for implementation, and one would be parked.

What happened to the Shapers and their ideas?
– One of the ideas was adopted and added to the Amdocs product roadmap.
– Another influenced management to make a company acquisition.
– The third is being explored at a leading technical institute.
– And the final idea is being built on further before take-off.

The Shapers are now well known at Amdocs. They are giving company-wide lectures and serving as mentors for the next generation of Shapers 2.0.

6 Development Cycle, Agile Process, Innovation Process

> Learn from yesterday, live for today, hope for tomorrow. The important thing is not to stop questioning.
> —Albert Einstein

Now, it is time to dig into the relationship between the development process and the innovation process. Not the easiest topic for sure. I will try answer the question of how to build upon one another by going through the most popular tools: simplified innovation (stage-gate) process, design thinking, lean startup, design sprint and the startup corporation.

In theory, the oldest and most common (in the past, at least), simplified innovation process looks as shown in Figure 6.1. It can be described in five stages and it can have decision gates in between, or it could be done more smoothly with only one decision when all stakeholders need to meet. During the other stages, an idea can be killed at any time by the person responsible for innovation (innovation manager) who triggers all stakeholders. The first decision gate (filter) has the crucial task of scanning and quickly filtering ideas by type, and eliminating known ideas and those who don't fit to the portfolio (or possible portfolio extension). The second decision gate (decision) opens up the question of value capture – what is the effort needed to make the idea happen and what is the value to capture? Is the value bigger than the effort, and could the idea lead to a successful project? If the idea gets approval from stakeholders, it will get the budget to be realised.

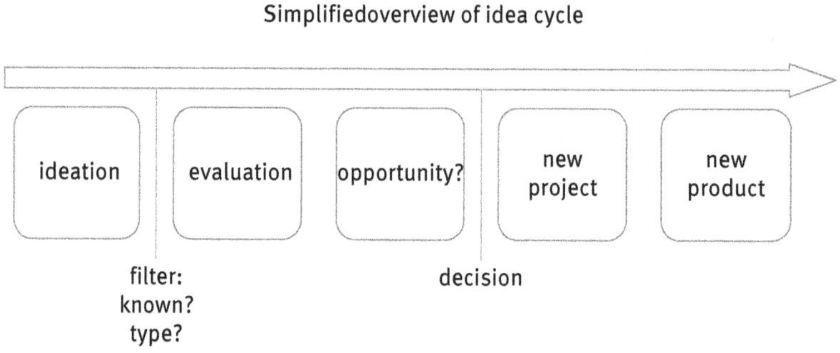

Simplifiedoverview of idea cycle

Figure 6.1: Simplified overview of an idea cycle.

How should this process be implemented in IT companies? Could it be embedded in agile? Adapted to design thinking? Improved by lean startup methodology?
The answer to all these questions is YES!

https://doi.org/10.1515/9783110654448-006

A short and fast development cycle in a software development ecosystem requires ideas that bring quick results. This is not easy and sometimes not achievable, but could be adapted to reflect the needs of the future.

To anyone who hasn't got agile experience, I always cite the example of making a cake: if you want to understand what agile means, make a cake, from start to the finish, with all parts of the process. This is a micro project that has all phases. First, you plan the project, scan resources and buy them if necessary. Next, you plan all tasks and then realise them in order. At the end, the cake must be decorated (marketing) and properly stored before everyone can see and eat it.

As I mentioned before, during these years I was working in a waterfall system, which was later replaced by an agile system. I must mention that the agile system was always heavily adapted to a special case. Let's say that every software department has its own kind of agile methodology and sometimes it's even a mix of agile and waterfall principles.

Figure 6.2 shows three lines that represent three types of possible project lifecycles:
-   Software development project lifecycle with its iterations (sprints).
-   Innovation project lifecycle which implements design thinking, lean startup and agile.
-   Software innovation project lifecycle where design thinking acts as part of ideation, lean startup is part of the decision process and agile methodology is part of project management and realisation of the idea.

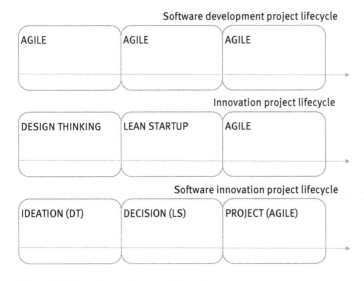

Figure 6.2: Three types of project lifecycles.

So, could design thinking, lean startup or agile be a part of the innovation process or the life of the product?

Every start of an innovation initiative is done in a similar way (need, followed by idea or problem and, finally, a solution). Could design thinking be part of it?

Design thinking

Post-its and meetings are often not the most favourite things in the world for the average software developer who likes to be left in peace in front of her screen (more on this in the chapter "Introverts as the Majority"). Hence, this approach should be done carefully, as many elements of design thinking can still be implemented. In my experience, design thinking steps should be adapted (as shown in Figure 6.3):

Empathise – understand the challenge – the creators of an innovation initiative, and later all participants in that initiative, must understand the problem. The problem can come from the customer, market or internally, but someone must be able to shape it.

Define – define the problem to solve – the goal of an innovation project, challenge or initiative must be understandable. It must be presented briefly, avoiding deep technical terminology and explanations. Participators must understand the challenge and feel that they are able to answer it. The problem must be defined in such a way that the company can solve it.

Ideate – brainstorm for a solution – each company must find the best way to brainstorm that best fit to their people (more in the chapters "Brainstorming as an Ideation Tool" and "Life After Brainstorming"), sometimes this is no brainstorming at all, but a special methodology that has been invented to best fit the environment.

Prototype – create a prototype to test the solution – fast prototype in order to (re)shape the idea. As this is done during the very first stages of the lifecycle, the prototype must be done really quickly; sometimes it may be just one PowerPoint slide.

Test – to improve the solution – the prototype is then tested when presented to the audience, which should help with the new reshaping of the idea.

This shortened and over-simplified approach can't be called design thinking, but maybe we could say that it is a "special company's 'designthinkingisation' of the first part of the innovation (or product) process" by putting user experience at the front. In short, this method should test the way customers use a certain product and then find a way to identify current and future needs (features).

Tip: developers will always like whiteboards more than post-its.

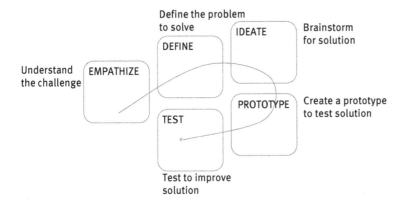

Figure 6.3: Design thinking.

Lean startup

In his book, *The Lean Startup,* Eric Ries explained how continuous innovation should be done and how it can be a part of the whole process in a company. Inside companies, it should become a mindset, not a process.

As presented in Figure 6.2 ("Three types of project lifecycles"), we can see the second step of the innovation process. It follows "design thinking", which resulted with an idea, which has already been reshaped after the first round of prototyping and testing. Now, it is time to decide whether the idea should be realised or not in a reasonable time frame.

Build – first build upon the current idea – make the minimum viable product in order to start learning. Eric Ries defines MVP as:

> The minimum viable product is that version of a new product which allows a team to collect the maximum amount of validated learning about customers with the least effort.[33]

Measure – monitor and analyse data in order to get results that will show the potential of the idea.

Learn – test, involve product owners, cross-functional teams, customers, or those who are close to customers to close your learning curve with a decision about the product (code).

And, if necessary, iterate the process.

It is not enough to present this methodology; it has to be adapted to the required organisation, department or even team. Internal coaches and facilitators could make this fun and try to bring this method closer to employees to make them internal entrepreneurs, trying to autonomously design their own minimum viable product (MVP).

---

33 https://www.agilealliance.org/glossary/mvp.

In contrast to agile, lean provides the opportunity to approach the customer in a different way, before the start of the project. It should also reduce risk and reduce the budget needed for individual innovation projects.

For software projects, this method could be presented as in Figure 6.4, with a build-measure-learn cycle adapted to **build through ideas – measure all the data – learn and code**.

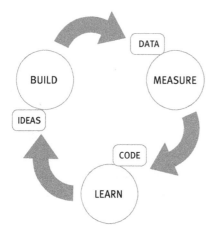

Figure 6.4: Lean startup.

Pivoting – changing strategic direction – is for me the most important part of this method. It is impossible to pivot without vision, as a pivot is a change in strategy without a change in vision.[34] There are many examples of pivoting. Nintendo was making playing cards and toys before starting with electronic games; Paypal was developing security software for handheld devices before switching to online payments; and Instagram was started as a check-in service similar to Foursquare.

There are several aspects that make this approach unique. For startups it is necessary to know how this small company can prosper, or what is needed to make their product visible or unique. Then this must be tested in the fastest and cheapest way. The key to success is learning from every experiment and then starting over (this is the build-measure-learn loop shown in Figure 6.4). If necessary, it should be possible to pivot and change strategy, or to stay on course – if it is the right direction.

In established companies, this principle could be adapted to smaller or bigger teams of intrapreneurs who could make their own startup inside the company or a "lean startup" as part of the usual innovation process.

---

34 Eric Ries: The Startup Way: How Modern Companies Use Entrepreneurial Management to Transform Culture and Drive Long-Term Growth, Currency (October 17, 2017).

In a larger organisation, the executive sponsor must be senior enough to clear obstacles, but not too senior to be unable to meet with individual teams.   –Eric Ries[35]

Design sprint

Design sprints are short and quick, with a focus on fast development and testing. They are highly recommended for the software development process, as the technique was born in such an environment.

A **design sprint** [36] is a fast, five-phase (and five day) process which uses design thinking aimed at creating a new product or feature by reducing risk.

The process help teams in understanding and defining goals, validating ideas and testing them. The design process is similar to sprints in an agile development cycle.

1. **Understand:** What is the problem and where to focus?
2. **Diverge:** Find solutions and sketch them.
3. **Converge:** Decide on a solution and plan the prototype.
4. **Prototype:** Design a prototype that can be tested.
5. **Test:** Testing with real users.

The sprints provide great power by fast-forwarding to the future to see the finished product and customer reactions, before making any expensive commitments.[37] It is a way to get insights about the product built as a realistic prototype on day four. Of course, success also depends on the strength and diversity of the design sprint, how you manage it and what action will follow it.

Give a good idea to a mediocre team, and they'll find a way to screw it up. Give a mediocre idea to a good team, and they'll find a way to make it better.[38]   –Daniel Coyle

The startup corporation

In their book, *The Innovation Paradox – Why Good Businesses Kill Breakthroughs and How They Can Change,*[39] Tony Davila and Marc J. Epstein coined the term "Startup Corporation":

---

35 Eric Ries: The Startup Way: How Modern Companies Use Entrepreneurial Management to Transform Culture and Drive Long-Term Growth, Currency (October 17, 2017).

36 The Design Sprint, GV – https://www.gv.com/sprint/.

37 Jake Knapp, John Zeratsky, Braden Kowitz: Sprint: How to Solve Big Problems and Test New Ideas in Just Five Days, Simon & Schuster; 1 edition (March 8, 2016).

38 Daniel Coyle: The Culture Code, The Secrets of Highly Successful Groups, Random House Audio; Unabridged edition (January 30, 2018).

39 Tony Davila and Marc J. Epstein: The Innovation Paradox, Why good businesses kill breakthroughs and they could change, Berrett-Koehler Publishers, Inc. 2014.

> The Startup Corporation is a set of management tools inspired by the way startup ecosystems are designed for exploration that allows established organizations to leverage their resources. In other words, the Startup Corporation emphasizes the strengths of startups when it comes to developing breakthroughs, but spotlights the strengths of established organizations when it comes to scaling and execution.

This is a set of management tools, which uses **the strengths of startups to innovate** and the **resources, network and ability of established companies to execute**. This combination should be a new engine for corporations, which could find a way to reinvent themselves.

> The Startup Corporation provides organisational tools to manage strategic discoveries – breakthrough innovations resulting from the combination of the insight of people throughout an organisation and its networks.

One recent study explained that the "winning formula for building new businesses combines the methods and pace of successful tech startups with the scale of long-standing companies[40]".

On the other hand, startups are often founded by former corporate employees who haven't been heard or haven't been given any (or enough) resources to follow their ideas. Then they start their own companies with more or less corporate knowledge, which could be crucial in surviving the first stage of a startup's life. The experience from corporate life could provide elements of corporate culture, its processes and life-stages to startups, even in its early stages, which ultimately could lead the way to the creation of a bigger, successful company.

Later, I will add examples of companies that use lean startup, design thinking and the concept of the Startup Corporation. For now, let's get back to the first way of handling innovation processes: a common, but a bit old-fashioned stage-gate process.

Example of the stage-gate process: An IT company from the communication, technology and media sector and their innovation ecosystem

(I haven't named the company, as it was recently bought and integrated into a new environment; however, the example of the innovation process is very interesting.)

The multinational company, with 2,000 people (mostly engineers) in several European countries, China and India, had a business scope which included

---

40 Philipp Hillenbrand, Dieter Kiewell, Rory Miller-Cheevers, Ivan Ostojic and Gisa Springer: Traditional company, new businesses: The pairing that can ensure an incumbent's survival, McKinsey and Company, June 2019.

products, services and solutions in telecommunications, media and aerospace. The organisational challenge was to answer the question: How to set up an innovation ecosystem in a knowledge-based technological experts' organisation to develop and market an innovative solution and product portfolio?[41]

It was clear that employees had know-how in telecommunications and media technologies and proven skills and expertise to quickly resolve technical issues. The company had the support of an internal system of networks dealing with specific topics and the means to search and find the required expertise quickly throughout the organisation. It was an internal technology management platform, which helped in the creation of groups of experts, but also the education system through the company.

Innovation culture was strongly supported and developed throughout the organisation. Main activities included top management attention – innovation was given a high priority and the current status of innovation activities was an integral part of employee events and quarterly newsletters. An innovation managers network was established with innovation managers available in all countries and business units. They strongly supported bottom-up innovation, questioning aspects of customer benefit, market situation, technical feasibility, strategic fit ... Innovation management as a central function in headquarters developed this process further and drove global initiatives. They coordinated all innovation activities and supported the exchange of best practices. An award system was done in a simple and transparent way, with contributors collecting points throughout the year and then being rewarded on broadcasted events. Information about the innovation process was available on intranet, together with news on innovation successes. Workshops were applied all over the company using various idea generation methods. Other forms of events such as "meet the sales" or "business talks" were held in order to bring information about the market directly to the employees.

Innovation management covered the early phase of idea handling or front end of innovation. Later stages, after the decision to fund the innovation project, were handled by project management, product lifecycle management or sales processes.

It is important to say that the evaluation of an idea was done by a global network of experts (in a stage of "review"). If the result was positive, the business unit in whose portfolio the idea best fit was assigned to proceed with that idea.

Here is the overview of the decision-gate innovation process:

Decision Gate 0: Creator submits ideas

Decision Gate 1: Idea accepted for further review and assignment to business unit

Decision Gate 2: Business unit adopts the idea

---

41 Hans-Jürgen August, Tomislav Buljubašić: Setting up an Innovation Ecosystem Supporting a New Organization's Strategy, The XXIII ISPIM Conference – Action for Innovation: Innovating from Experience – in Barcelona, Spain.

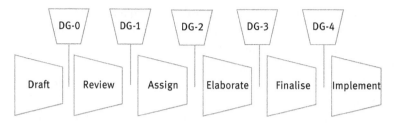

Figure 6.5: Overview of innovation process with decision gates.

Decision Gate 3: Ready for decision by top management

Decision Gate 4: Decision on innovation project including funding by top management

Shortcut: Proposals accepted by business units head enter the process at DG-2

The success of an innovation programme was best seen by the number of ideas employees submitted directly to the innovation portal (company-wide idea generation platform).

Quick decision-making using the stage-gate process was essential for further success; it required detailed preparation of the decision proposal using a common set of templates, including a standardised business case calculation form. The network of innovation managers in the company was coached and gained experience through the process, which was necessary for gaining speed during this phase of the process.

The attention and commitment of top management and, at the end, the willingness to make a decision, opened the way to the success of the process. Another point in the company's success was that technology management and innovation strategy were communicated as parts of the operational units' strategies. In addition, every employee had personal support for development and submission of ideas by a network of innovation managers.

Personal decision meetings, even in early stages, accelerated the processing of ideas and in some cases even led to new ideas. This made the process transparent and successful for all stakeholders. Key points were:

- proper preparation of decision proposals
- coaching by the innovation managers
- proposal reviews
- top management availability

7 Reward Programme and Effects of Rewarding

> If we were motivated by money, we would have sold the company a long time ago and ended
> up on a beach.　　　　　　　　　　　　　　　　　　　　　　　　　　　　　　– Larry Page

In my former company, there were several different innovation reward systems during the span of 10 years. Some of these reward systems were company-wide methodologies, but some were only local and affected only some entities. I will focus on the analysis and how these different approaches affected the innovation culture of the organisation.

Several innovation awarding systems were used during that time, and all metrics kept track of the changes in the innovation ecosystem. The formula-based incentive system for incremental innovations was the only constant in this timeframe.

It is important to mention that my colleagues were software developers working in the telecommunications and multimedia sector.

Monetary vs. non-monetary awarding

Monetary vs. non-monetary rewarding is often a topic of debates in innovation management literature. The common belief is that innovators are not guided by money. Non-monetary awards, such as recognition in the organisation and the actual realisation of ideas, are usually considered more important.

Employees are motivated to do things for which they have a passion, so such topics could be identified or others presented in such a way. Engineers always want to work on the latest technologies and this will make them passionate. To achieve that, every topic could be linked to the latest technology and presented in a way to increase interest in the initiative.

Self-motivation is crucial for creativity and people who are motivated only by rewards will create only incremental ideas needed to get the reward – that is surely not the desired output for any innovation manager. If people are triggered only by rewards, they will lose their focus on ideas in the crucial stages of their lifecycle. Also, they will not be able to kill their idea or leave it to die.

Reward systems

Many companies have an award system, but also a large number of companies don't offer incentives – those are mostly the ones that don't have innovation system at all. An important incentive that should be highlighted is surely the dedicated time for innovation, as this could be more important for the future of an idea and its innovator.

https://doi.org/10.1515/9783110654448-007

Over a period of eight years, several innovation programmes were present inside the observed company. Some were company-wide programmes and some were oriented only toward a business unit or particular entity:

– Company-wide improvement programme: Company-wide programme where money awards are given for successful improvements (formula-based system for awarding), mostly process improvements.

– Bonus programme: Yearly award for the 10 best innovators in our entity with money awards, but innovators also had the opportunity to present their ideas in front of management and other award-winners, as well in front of the whole company (intranet). All realised ideas were presented internally via intranet and on specially printed brochures celebrating all innovators and their ideas. This programme was in use for four years and is explained in the chapter "Igniting the Innovation Process".

– Innovation challenges: Call for innovations for the defined topic, short duration (two weeks) in which all employees are called to submit ideas. The call comes directly from the management. Innovation workshops are held in parallel, in which invited colleagues get additional help in finding or shaping ideas. No awards, but the best ideas have the chance to be funded. Everyone in the company gets the mail with the call and anyone can submit an idea, whether she is invited to a special workshop or not. This initiative is further elaborated in the chapter "Innovation Challenges".

– Innovation awards: This was a company-wide award programme. Employees submitting innovation ideas, inventions and improvement proposals collected points. The best contributors were rewarded regularly during an event that was broadcasted globally. Rewards were tech gadgets (smartphones, tablets, laptops) or travel vouchers.

Measurements

To be able to make a conclusion, I must focus on two main parameters for measurement:

– number of submitted ideas per employee, divided by improvement ideas and innovation (business idea) proposals
– number of employees with idea(s)

To get a result about the influence of rewarding systems, all rewarding systems must be compared as in Figure 7.1. The question of which reward system delivers the best results is based on the number of new idea submissions, the number of submitters and the quality of ideas connected with the innovation strategy of the organisation.

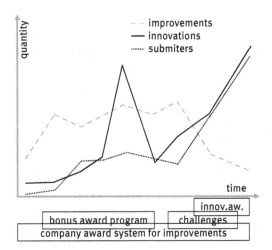

Figure 7.1: Numbers of improvement ideas, innovation proposals and the number of submitters and reward systems per year.

Measurement results were taken from the company innovation portal (a tool for handling innovation processes, accessible to everyone internally), where all ideas are submitted and tracked. It is important to emphasise that many ideas proposed in innovation workshops or during innovation challenges, which were rejected during the first evaluation, were not submitted to the company innovation portal and are not included in this analysis.

Each rewarding system had a quick response for the all studied data, but with many complex behaviours, such as an increase (or not) in the quality of ideas and the response from innovators and management.

It is also clear that without special programmes (monetary or non-monetary – depending on the kind of ideas needed), all presented data begin to fall dramatically.

So, it can be said that monetary awarding leads to a quick and strong response in regard to innovation in an organisation, but is it enough and is it what one wants to achieve? Many other small steps must be taken to achieve the necessary results and raise or maintain the level of innovation culture. On the other hand, non-monetary awarding implemented in innovation challenges produces a high number of ideas, but not of the required quality if the topic is too broad or not well defined. A combination of both systems proved to be best, with the implementation of a yearly innovation award contest and non-monetary innovation challenges with narrow topics. This leads new ideas with the desired quality, but also maintains the flow of incremental ideas. To achieve the best result, the reward system has to be in alignment with the innovation culture and with the current strategy of the organisation.

The data obtained confirms that incremental ideas are more strongly connected with incentives and that semi-radical and radical innovations are more connected with recognition as an award. The number of incremental ideas always increased after the introduction of a new reward system. Incremental ideas always exist in the software company, but the question is whether these ideas would be inserted into the innovation process. Rewards provide the necessary push for submitters to actually describe their ideas and to share them with the whole organisation.

One can also see that the number of semi-radical and radical ideas was connected with the number of innovation workshops. Topic-oriented innovation workshops produced a large number of ideas and the reward system didn't affect the number of ideas. However, the quality of these ideas is not always on a high level and a reward system (not necessarily monetary) could help to trigger innovators to think about their ideas outside of workshops as well. To achieve this, innovators must be equipped with the needed information about the topic or even with the innovation strategy of the department, entity or company.

In the case of radical ideas, the best reward for an innovator is recognition which includes company-wide news about the successful idea or presentation in a yearly award gala ceremony. The presentation of successful ideas in front of colleagues and/or management always means praise for an innovator. The biggest praise is, of course, the realisation of the idea.

The results illustrate the experiences we had during a span of eight years and deepens the current understanding of this topic. Innovators should be praised not only with extrinsic rewards, but also with recognition inside the organisation and a celebration of successful ideas.

This example shows that the best results for business ideas (innovations) are achieved by using quick, responsive, short innovation contests (challenges) where many colleagues can participate and get a quick response from experts because the subject is a narrow topic.

Improvement ideas, on the other hand, need a long lasting-programme, which praises the innovators and offers awards such as money or gadgets. Many improvements will not be submitted to an innovation programme and will not be recognised as ideas if the improvement programme does not have awards. Improvement ideas are everywhere, in every company; the only difference between entities is whether improvements are evaluated and awarded.

The number of people involved in innovation is the best reflection on the state of innovation culture in a company. In the scope of this analysis, we can see that this number was increased with the bonus award programme, but later innovation challenges raised the number even more. Both programmes reached everyone in the organisation, as they were communicated via mail and via intranet news.

The connection between raising an innovation culture and topic-oriented innovation workshops, with a chance for everyone to be part of the contest, led to the best results in this example.[42]

The influence of rewards and an innovation culture on the state of innovation in an organisation is shown in Figure 7.2.

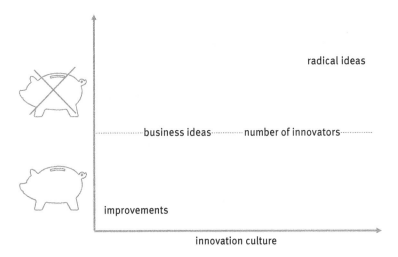

Figure 7.2: Rewarding systems.

To summarise, when observing bottom-up ideas in an organisation, it can be said that the number of improvements depends on monetary awards, but the number of business ideas does not necessarily depend on them. Innovators are also driven by other non-monetary and intrinsic rewards such as recognition and, most importantly, the final realisation of the idea. A number of innovators are surely influenced by the state of innovation culture. In the end, radical ideas can appear only in if there is a high level of innovation culture in the organisation and a well-established innovation process supported from all levels inside the company.

Figure 7.3 shows the answers from a survey about the motivation of developers according to innovation.

Most respondents said that they are motivated by the implementation of the idea (55%). Twenty percent are motivated by being honoured publicly inside their organisation (events, intranet news, speeches, presentations); 20% are motivated by rewards as attending conferences or taking external trainings; and only 5% are motivated by being selected for future innovation programmes. The last point shows that the

---

42 Tomislav Buljubašić, "Establishing Innovative Culture", PODIM Conference, Maribor, Slovenia, April 2010.

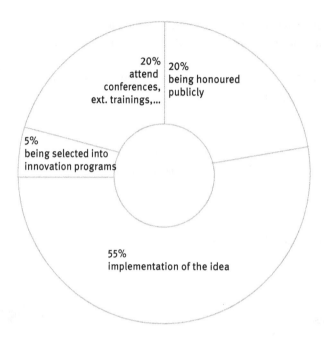

Figure 7.3: Motivation of developers.

surveyed company lacks an innovation culture, but all other answers are common for a software development environment. Software developers simply do not care too much about attention, they just want to get their work (ideas) done (implemented).

Igniting a new programme – rewarding

Starting an innovation process is easier if it is supported with rewards. Rewards will ignite employees who are not moved by innovation initiatives (intrinsically motivated) alone, and rewards must be carefully managed in a way that makes the innovation process more important in the eyes of some colleagues. This should support innovation responsible in changing the company's innovation climate and must be carefully prepared from the top, whether every the realization of every idea is rewarded or just the best x number of innovators with the highest number of yearly points. Rewards could be gadgets, money, share in the future success of an idea or one time reward. Human resource officers could be a great help when establishing such a system.

Time to implement ideas inside the organisation could also be considered a kind of reward. For some innovators, this time (outside their daily projects) could be the best prize. Seed funding of a project that could become an internal startup or spin-off could also be considered as a reward. This is a necessary help that always pushes projects forward.

In startups, it is common to reward employees with equity stake and these employees will then have additional motivation to make the company prosperous. Such a principle could be mapped to the innovation system in a medium-sized or big company in a way that innovator could get a reward as a percentage of the profit that her innovation made in first x number of years. This could make an innovator wealthy, but also bring additional attention to innovation activities from a large portion of employees that are motivated extrinsically.

8 Brainstorming as an Ideation Tool

Two heads are definitely better than one and by sourcing ideas from each other, you have a better chance of coming up with a strategy that will allow your business to overcome a setback or challenge. — Richard Branson

It's always a challenge to bring the innovative culture of any organisation to a higher level. After the promotion of innovation programme and removing the barriers, one of the tasks connected with that challenge is to be successful in the idea generation. The focus can be on the number of ideas, but it is also always expected to reach a certain quality to be able to get results in the end.

When trying to get quality ideas aligned with a company portfolio and the situation on the market, three different approaches can be combined: traditional brainstorming (sometimes connected with idea awareness workshops), innovation task force meetings and an internal open contest for ideas.

Traditional brainstorming is well known for its principles and rules. Certainly, most principles can be used in many business sectors, but some must be put in front depending on the particular needs of the sector. In the case of software development, as I saw it, participants of idea generation workshops are highly skilled professionals with extensive knowledge of their product, but without detailed information about the market or competition. Often, they know only some parts of their product and don't have an overview of a complete ecosystem in which their product (or even the company) lives.

Good preparation is essential for success; the topic for which ideas are needed should be as narrow as possible and explained well at the start of a brainstorming session, or even in the request sent to participants together with an invitation to the workshop. This explanation should contain a current overview of customers and competitors on the selected topic, together, with the latest trends in this topic. A small presentation before the workshop will get participants involved in the topic.

By observing the changes and reflecting on different idea generation principles, it can be seen that only workshops which are focused on a selected topic from the beginning can achieve clear results. From my experience, the quantity of incremental ideas that are generated in comparison with realised incremental ideas speaks that every department has the opportunity for improvements and savings. That affects every area of software development, project management or testing. In contrary, radical of semi-radical ideas have fewer chances, even as the number of these ideas is sometimes big. To be successful with radical ideas, many connections must be established throughout the company; the most important is with sales, strategy and portfolio development. With that in mind, brainstorming should be focused on one kind of idea. Incremental and radical ideas shouldn't be mixed. If you are aiming high, just do it and ask participants for radical ideas.

https://doi.org/10.1515/9783110654448-008

The brainstorming principle should be praised and upgraded with other methods to create the needed results. This includes some kind of innovation contest that can last throughout the year or just the request with a short timeframe for ideas about a narrow topic like an internal innovation contest.

In short, the brainstorming method should be expanded with other initiatives to get the best results. "What if" cards, future scenarios or time machine visions could start the thinking and then all creative paths in a session should be multiplied and directed.

I saw that developers don't like post-its and if you put them in the room and give them a bunch of yellow stickers, they would not feel too good and they would not collaborate in the right way. So, the workshop may be done without sticking notes to the walls. Working in groups, defer judgement and try to generate as many ideas as possible to show sceptical persons that this can work. Maybe not everyone will be engaged, but ideas can still be born in series.

You will always note several types of characters in brainstorming workshops. First, the ones that are really engaged and interested. The second group are people that will not say a word because they have hidden motives. Maybe they are angry at superiors, thinking of quitting or maybe they don't want anyone else to hear their idea. The third group are people who are too introverted to join a discussion; they will listen, but not say anything. Work in a group can get them to talk a little, but don't expect much.

In order to have successful innovation projects, innovators have to be identified and those who are too quiet in workshops must have another option to join innovation initiatives.

9 Life After Brainstorming

> Some people see innovation as change, but we have never really seen it like that. It's making things better.
> –Tim Cook

Brainstorming is not dead. It is adapted and still used when necessary, but it is not the main ideation technique as in the past. Its place is taken by other methods where brainstorming is embedded in one part of the process or by an adapted innovation challenge with ideation methods that every company adjusts in their way.

In my case, brainstorming was replaced with redesigned innovation campaigns for a special environment where a traditional brainstorming approach was simply not working. Running innovation campaigns in a software development company is often a big challenge and from the experience of 50+ events, I learned that many participants were simply not involved enough in the discussion. Idea generation and the quality of ideas were also not on the level we needed. Experience also showed that colleagues were not motivated with rewards, but with trendy and inspirational topics which had more chances for the future success of ideas.

The key was in shaping short, well-described topics using web-based tools, which allows transparency and building on the ideas of others. We were focused on efforts to adapt our approach. In the end, we got a much higher participation level and most important, enhanced quality of ideas. The next steps, evaluation and presenting of ideas before realisation, was now simpler and easier to prepare both to idea owners and to evaluators.

The result illustrates the experience of this adapted methodology, which is part of the front-end-of-innovation topic. With this new approach, we succeeded in reaching a target in a short-term innovation contest and most of all, in increasing the participation level and raise innovation awareness company-wide, which also has an impact on the level of innovation culture.

This approach is tailor-made and adapted for the software-oriented company and it is described in the chapter "Innovation Challenges" and further explained in the chapter "7innovation Method".

Use of brainstorming

Brainstorming has not been fully abandoned; it is used as self-brainstorming – a method for every individual who will ask herself about the topic or the problem stated in the innovation challenge. The innovation manager must periodically remind people of the topic and give further stimuli for brainstorming to all participants. In that way, brainstorming is leaving corporate offices and coming to buses, cars, streets and homes, everywhere where participants will be. It is a big plus if innovators know about brainstorming technique and uses its rules on themselves.

https://doi.org/10.1515/9783110654448-009

Encourage wild ideas, stay focused on the topic, be visual, go for quantity – these rules also work great when brainstorming is done alone. Education about brainstorming technique could be a part of an innovation awareness workshop, which should be held all over the company when starting innovation activities.

Tools

There are so many ideation tools existing right now. The Florence Innovation Project[43] lists 565 methods and tools. This project was formed around the question: "How do I find the best method for my current innovation challenge without having to read many different books each time?" Of course, only a fraction of these methods are needed when implementing an innovation programme in the organisation. Ultimately, the set of tools could be narrowed to 3–5 methods, but some methods from the list could be parked for special purposes if needed for specific challenges or customer workshops.

Types of corporate innovation programmes

In a report, "The corporate innovation: How large corporations avoid disruption by strengthening their ecosystem",[44] the authors Owyang and Szymansky wrote about the frequency of the top 10 types of corporate innovation programmes. Number one is having a **dedicated innovation team** (79%), followed by an **innovation "centre of excellence"** (61%), an inclusive programme that brings together multiple departments with the goal of standardising and scaling innovation across entire organisations. It is followed by **technology education/university publishing** (54%), **intrapreneur programmes** (51%) and **startup investments** (49%). The next type is **innovation tours** (49%), as a way to train corporate leaders by taking tours of startups and businesses that are leading the way in a market or topic. At the bottom are **external accelerator partnerships** (40%), **startup acquisitions** (39%) and **open innovation** (35%).

Which of these types best fits software firms, and which of these innovation programmes could ignite innovation success in a time of (market and technology) change?

Having a dedicated innovation team is one way to bring together experts, idea-makers and market specialists, and it surely can fit in a large percentage of companies. Some

---

43 https://www.ask-flip.com https://www.verrocchio-institute.com/en/.
44 Report entitled "The corporate innovation imperative: How large corporations avoid disruption by strengthening their ecosystem," by authors Jeremiah Owyang and Jaimy Szymanski from the organisation Crowd Companies.
  https://venturebeat.com/2017/02/17/10-ways-companies-are-looking-at-driving-innovation/.

small companies or startups are run in such a way that the whole company is a kind of innovation team. Later the leader must carefully choose associates as the company grows, so as not to lose the innovation magic.

A centre of excellence can be seen as a way to make a full-scale innovation programme in the company, but it can also go in the wrong direction of operational control – the opposite of the freedom that innovation needs in an organisation.

An intrapreneur programme (corporate entrepreneurship) is something that can be established in any entity with a clear goal of making everyone visible and ready to ideate. An essential part of every intrapreneurship programme is the help people get after ideation: how will they make it in the company's environment? What sort of help can they get? An innovation ecosystem must be built as a frame around intrapreneurship programme providing innovator with business process and product methodology or simply adding the right coordinator to guide or lead the project if innovator gets only partial role in it. Education about tools and processes must support the programme.

Opening up to hackathons or internal incubators provided for externals could be a great source of recruiting new employees, but also for including new ideas from a fresh outsider's look at internal projects, products or visions. Newcomers or students can often bring a new perspective to companies, which are closed in their shell and must be taken as a part of innovation efforts.

Startup acquisitions and investments are something that many companies consider, but maybe they should think instead of changing their thinking so it is more like a startup to be able to quickly change directions (pivot).

The best way of starting to change a company is to know your company and your colleagues. Then it's easy to pick the right tool or type of innovation initiative to achieve success. Hence, a kind of audit or survey could be a quick way to save effort, better than building an unnecessary programme.

Now, let's look at an example of a big IT company with several innovation streams and a company-wide innovation challenge with intrapreurship, education, special kits and awards.

Example: Cisco's Innovate Everywhere Challenge

Cisco, the worldwide leader in IT, networking, and cybersecurity solutions with 25,000 engineers and more than 19,000 patents already enjoys a rich history of high-tech innovation.

They define innovation[45] as creating something significantly new, better and of value. Their innovation engine is composed of five key pillars:
1. Build – use organic innovation from engineering teams.

---

45 https://newsroom.cisco.com/feature-content?articleId=1720841.

2. Buy – acquire companies with a technology complementary to business priorities.
3. Partner – create solutions and go-to-market strategy with technology and services partners.
4. Invest – make direct and indirect investments in promising startups, entrepreneurs and venture funds.
5. Co-develop – work with customers, leading innovators and decision-makers on new, industry-changing ideas built on the network.

The main question is how to think and act like a startup, but scale as an enterprise, as at one time every organisation was a startup.

Cisco's Innovate Everywhere Challenge (shown in Figure 9.1) encouraged every employee to "team up, disrupt and innovate".[46] The key objectives of the Innovate Everywhere Challenge were to:
- capture disruptive venture ideas from Cisco employees and help grow them
- create game-changing value for customers, partners, and employees
- develop entrepreneurship skills and culture at Cisco
- enhance employee experience, empowerment and collaboration across all functions
- reinforce Cisco's "innovator" brand to attract, develop and retain talent

Forty-eight percent of their workforce, and every single function, was engaged in the challenge in some way. More than 2,000 employees submitted more than 1,100 ideas, with nearly 50% of the submissions were from teams. More than 18,000 employees from 50 countries participated in the challenge community and employees made more than 4,000 comments and cast more than 45,000 votes.

In the six months after the competition launched, evaluations from more than 250 judges and votes from employees chose six finalist teams from more than 1,100 entries. Finalists then pitched their ventures to a panel of industry leaders from inside and outside the company in the 90-minute grand finale which was broadcast companywide. Two days later, the challenge's three winners were announced at Cisco's regularly scheduled meeting for all employees and the winning teams received the tools they needed to implement their ideas. These included three months of time-off, $50,000 ($25,000 in seed funds and $25,000 in recognition), corporate concierge services to help remove roadblocks, extensive technology resources and mentors.

To ensure that momentum continued throughout the competition, the organisers developed adventure kits for everyone and held a three-day boot camp for the 15 semi-finalists to introduce them to the world of lean startups, where ventures are tested, validated, and advanced. Adventure Kits were inspired by Adobe Kickbox

---

46 Innovate Everywhere Challenge White Paper: Cisco Ignites Companywide Startup Culture, 2016. https://newsroom.cisco.com/documents/10157/1781523/2019_WhitePaper_Final_CMRG6.pdf.

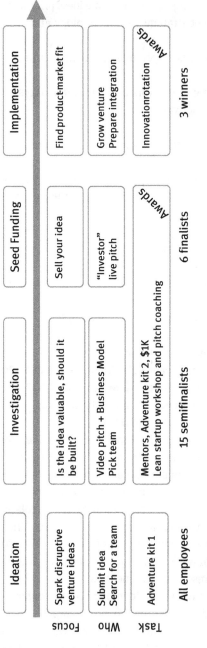

	Ideation	Investigation	Seed Funding	Implementation
Focus	Spark disruptive venture ideas	Is the idea valuable, should it be built?	Sell your idea	Find product-market fit
Who	Submit idea Search for a team	Video pitch + Business Model Pick team	"Investor" live pitch	Grow venture Prepare integration
Task	Adventure kit 1	Mentors, Adventure kit 2, $1K Lean startup workshop and pitch coaching	Awards	Innovation rotation Awards
	All employees	15 semifinalists	6 finalists	3 winners

Figure 9.1: Cisco's six-month timeline and process.

and they refined the programme through lessons learned from innovation pro-grammes at other Cisco organisations, and from the insights of industry leaders. Adventure Kit 1 provided a step-by-step guide for ideation and was action-oriented, focusing on four objectives visualised on 16 colourful cards. Adventure Kit 2 was an introduction to lean startup, as an effort created to innovate the right thing in less time with fewer resources.

As part of the "My Innovation" initiative, Cisco plans to continue accelerating the Innovate Everywhere Challenge to further foster entrepreneurial energy with priority on:

- Matchmaking network – future investments will focus on developing a more robust and comprehensive platform for entrepreneurs to find the right mix of skills, interests, functions, geographies and job rankings for teams.
- Speed-up challenges – the company will develop a series of different types of challenges on a more frequent basis, perhaps twice a year and compressing the ideate-to-incubate time cycle.
- Focus the challenge – the company is considering challenging employees with a specific problem statement. Essentially a challenge within the challenge.
- Founder and funder behaviours – each employee will get "virtual currency" to "invest" in venture ideas with the goal of progressively giving the crowd a larger role in the idea selection process.
- Innovation spaces – these are an established global network of innovation centres, but with teams that aren't always located in those cities, to capitalise on their resources; innovation spaces are now being planned on major Cisco campuses.
- Coaching and mentoring.

10 From Ideation to Realisation

> What I love about the creative process, and this may sound naive, but it is this idea that
> one day there is no idea, and no solution, but the next day there is an idea. I find that incredi-
> bly exciting and conceptually actually remarkable. — Jonathan Ive

After ideation, the critical point in every innovation programme is the realisation of
ideas. With that in mind, there are some challenges facing innovation implementation in a software development environment that must be pointed out now:
- space for experimenting
- middle management problem
- "sales doesn't listen to us"
- introverts are the majority (explained in the chapter "Introverts as the Majority?")
- short product cycle (explained in the chapter "Development Cycle, Agile Process,
  Innovation Process")
- specially adapted methodology (explained in the chapter "Innovation
  Challenges")
- listen to customers
- best practices
- bottom-up ideas
- develop entrepreneurship skills
- balance top-down and bottom-up ideas
- funding
- innovation leaders

Let's briefly take a look at these challenges.

Space for experimenting

Intrapreneurs should have time and other resources for experimenting.
Experimentation should not only be supported, but also encouraged. The path to successful innovation is always connected with many failures. To survive these failures,
an important part of corporate strategy must be resource allocation for the innovation
ecosystem and this must come from the top. As IT companies are living in agile
cycles, this is even harder and the biggest challenge is to get support to isolate innovators on innovation projects.

https://doi.org/10.1515/9783110654448-010

Middle managers

Is one of the biggest innovation barriers in the corporate world today how to convince middle managers to contribute to innovation? In his book, *Relentless Innovation*,[47] Jeffrey Phillips defines this problem as the following:

> In a world where so many factors are in flux, middle managers count on business as usual as a reliable, trustworthy way to get work done efficiently and effectively and they are therefore avid defenders of the model, often rejecting innovation.

In the process of establishing an innovation culture, or during an innovation campaign, many questions and comments can come from middle managers, such as:
- "We run our daily business and don't have time for new ideas".
- "How can you convince me that this idea will put us ahead of our competitors?"
- "The risk of failing is too high and we cannot avoid ourselves to lose time".
- "We have a product that sells well and only needs some improvements".
- "I can't see how a new idea can influence our daily work, as our work is based upon customer wishes".
- Even worse is when there is simply no answer.

So, how to convince them to become innovation evangelists?

Middle managers manage 20, 30, 50 or more direct reports and their day is never long enough. They are always at meetings and always busy. They often don't see the importance of innovation and don't like to disturb the current process. But their position shouldn't create a bottleneck and block idea initiatives.

Instead, middle managers could be in the centre of innovation activities, like decision-makers in the innovation process or presenters in ideation workshops or even starters of innovation campaigns. Once they are on the "side of Innovation", the company is on the way to realising innovations – new products – and to starting a powerful innovation machine from an already established innovation process.

They must allow their team members to be 100% focused and 100% dedicated to an innovation project, if needed. It is not enough to give innovators 50% of time because their daily job will take them away, or they will be doing innovation projects during overtime, which is not applicable. The other case is to dedicate innovators some days during the week (like Innovation Fridays) for innovation projects, but then it must be clear that they should not be disturbed with other tasks. This is often a big challenge.

---

47 Jeffrey Phillips: Relentless Innovation: What Works, What Doesn't – And What That Means For Your Business, McGraw-Hill Education 2011.

"Sales doesn't listen to us"

There is often a big gap between development and sales. Sales managers live in their own world with a focus on customers and market insights. Their world is so far away from the open spaces, cubicles or home offices of software developers who rarely see or hear a customer or any customer insights. These two worlds operate in the same environment – the same company, so it should not be impossible to get them on a common topic. They must be connected to product managers and other stakeholders in every development ecosystem, but is this connection something that encourages innovation? Often not. Often this leads to the next challenge ...

Listen to customers

Constantly listening to customers can lead in the wrong direction. Companies should not listen to what customers want, but watch what they do.

If you asked customers two decades ago whether they wanted a service with which they would be able to exchange 160-character text messages between mobile phones, they would have said: "What will we do with that? Well, it's easier to call a person". Reality has turned out completely differently with the great success of text messaging or SMS.

Gathering market insights and listening to customer wishes leads to incremental innovations and to new versions of existing products covering features that customers request. No radical changes, no new products, no new portfolio elements. What are customers' complaints? In B2C business, are they complaining on social media, websites, forums? Can someone check these complaints and single out those repeated over time?

In the B2B environment, a salesperson can help with insights or clear the way to reach the customer so as to help innovation teams. They can arrange a customer interview or customer innovation workshop. As they will be selling any future product, it is good to have their involvement and their opinions.[48] A **customer innovation workshop** should put customers, sales and technicians together and everyone should present their future scenario, regardless of whether it is six months, one year or five years in the future. This could be a nice way to start a conversation about existing products and their destiny on the market. The simpler way to get customer insights is a **customer interview**; it is the one-on-one talk where the customer has the opportunity to give feedback about the product. This could be started around a reported problem, common perspective or future features that are needed.

---

[48] Susana Jurado Apruzzese, Maria Olano Mata: Lean Elephants – Addressing the Innovation Challenge in Big Companies, Innovation and Research – Telefonica I+D, 2014.

The social game development company Zynga has a special kind of market testing method called "ghetto testing".[49] They use it to estimate the demand for new games. They post a teaser ad on a well-visited webpage and test the number of a potential customers by counting clicks. In this way, they assess customer demand without writing a line of code.

Best practices

A few times I have noticed that the biggest problem some development teams face is best practices. Sometimes teams import tools, methods and behaviours from other departments, or companies and rely upon them, even if these concepts are several years old.

The best practices, therefore, encourage ignorance of innovation. Reliance on proven methodologies leads to stability, but also to mediocrity. Only taking a risk and introducing the newest techniques can make the company different and, ultimately, innovative.

The biggest enemies, in this case, are micromanagers across the organisation that function in a way that the current system is set up. They simply act on autopilot, which gives them sense of security. On the other hand, innovation is the opposite; it provides no security and its outcome is unpredictable. Innovation should act as a breaker of rules and, if current practices don't support it, new practices must be set up.

Bottom-up ideas

Top-down innovations coming from management or the sales department often define the innovation culture inside a company. And often, this is everything companies do concerning this topic. It is much easier to leave ideas to that part of the company that has market insights, direct contact to customers and most importantly – the budget.

In that case, innovation is defined by the leaders of the company and is guided by just following the vision of the management. But to be successful and innovative, the company must enable everyone to contribute. Bottom-up ideas are more difficult to maintain, process and finance, but they are an important part of the future of every company and they should secure new improvements, incremental innovations and in the end new projects and visions.

---

49 Tom and David Kelley: Creative Confidence: Unleashing the Creative Potential within Us All, HARPER COLLINS (21 May 2015).

Successful companies must give the chance to every employee to be an entrepreneur or innovator. In short, bottom-up ideas can't flourish in a top-down company; this must be changed in order to set up a healthy innovation climate.

Develop entrepreneurship skills

Making entrepreneurs out of developers (or other persons) in software companies is a challenging task, but surely this is a must in order to have satisfied colleagues who really have the feeling that their ideas could live. This should be aligned with executives, human resources and sometimes with technology management. I will get back to this topic in the chapter "Every Engineer Needs a Businessman".

Balance top-down and bottom-up ideas

Bottom-up ideas are the goal of innovation initiatives; the goal of an innovation culture and every innovation manager should be fighting for them. Still, their chances are often lower than for top-down ideas and to keep the innovation process and initiatives alive we must balance them by supporting bottom-up ideas, as they should be part of the process, too.

Top-down ideas will create success stories which will also push future employee ideas in new directions and, in the end, realisation.

On the other hand, when the process becomes mature, there is a chance that innovation projects will have to fight for resources with other projects coming from the usual process. Because of that, it is necessary to equalise top-down and bottom-up innovation ideas (in later stages of projects) so that they have the same chance of getting the support they need. This is achievable only using innovation metrics and if all parts of the process are under control.

Funding

When ideas mature and reach a stage where they can be elaborated on in a quality style, they also reach a point where they can be stopped (or not) because of a simple reason – money. Funding must be available and allocated in the company in order to get the chance to most prosperous ideas. There should be no lower limit for funding ideas, as sometimes ideas don't need many resources to be realised. On the other hand, sometimes ideas need quite a lot (big budget) and all stakeholders must agree on spending a big part of the yearly idea budget on one innovation.

In organisations oriented toward incremental innovations and a top-down approach, it is possible that some ideas bypass the innovation system and are funded by a business unit budget – those ideas are certainly not recognised later as they are flying under the innovation radar. Another problem which could occur is when projects are funded with a big budget allocated for top-down ideas (even when ideas are not called "innovations", but "product enhancements"). Then "usual" bottom-up ideas which are coming through the system may be simply too small, and even when resources are allocated, ideas don't get much attention as the bigger top-down ideas get all the credit. I have seen examples of both cases and the crucial task rests again on the shoulders of innovation manager who must recognise all activities and praise them inside the innovation programme.

Turning to types of ideas and financing, it can be said that incremental ideas are often funded by business units, while the radical ideas are funded either directly by executives or by allocating the innovation budget. Strategic bets are tightly connected with the top-down approach; on the contrary, new product ideas can be bottom-up.[50]

Big companies also have the problems of no coordination, when some business units in the company are developing the same thing without knowing about the development in other parts of the company. Innovation should break this silo thinking and open up perspectives in big corporations. This can be done only by global transparency and coordination. Again, it's a task for technology management, innovation management, but also for those responsible for the portfolio and product.

Innovation leaders

Leading a company means thinking about its present and future. There is a much easier path toward innovation in any organisation if the leader understands, supports and funds the innovation process. This is a shortcut to success, but is it always achievable?

Company executives come to top-level positions because of their success in leading teams, departments, products or other organisations; there is rarely a situation in which someone is promoted to a top position only because of their creativity.

Many companies or startups are started as a vision of their founder; later, as the company grows, this person retains her place as a creative leader but must give the freedom to be creative also to other persons in the organisation. Simply put, a creative leader must be able to follow her own dreams, but also let others fulfil their inner urges for creativity.

---

50 Tony Davila, Marc J. Epstein: Innovation Paradox Why Good Businesses Kill Breakthroughs and How They Can Change, Berrett-Koehler Publishers; 1 edition (June 30, 2014).

Innovation leaders must provide a certain amount of space for innovation to flourish. By this I mean an innovation culture in an organisation which needs a budget, but also metrics using special key performance indicators which will not endanger innovation efforts, but keep the process measurable and on the right track. They should remove all barriers innovators might face in the organisation and enable them to focus on their innovation project.

Innovation hierarchy is often very flat and innovation managers often have the possibility of direct communication with executives; this option can be essential when starting innovation efforts.

In software development, an innovation environment is seen as the most usual thing that should happen with every project, but it is often put aside because of short-term goals that provide quick results and satisfy the customer (and company leaders, too). I have seen examples of stopping or postponing innovation programmes, but also of totally neglecting innovation for years in departments or organisations full of potential.

Innovation means experiments, prototypes, failures and education; it means uncertainty and leaders must be ready for it. When ideas are realised as innovations, these ideas must be championed and this is the task for leaders who must support innovators and make them visible inside the organisation in order to support others who will follow their path.

But what happens when your boss isn't convinced that innovation gets results or you have a new boss who is reluctant to continue or start an initiative?
First, maybe you'll have only one chance, so timing and preparation are crucial. Be sure to prepare all the benefits that an innovation programme will bring and how this will help the company in the (near) future. Maybe it will be easier to convince her by adding several examples from companies in the same market. Sketch or present a concrete example and try to include the executive in some role as well. Later, try to include the CEO on the innovation board, but also in other activities. This should make your boss an innovation supporter.

Are companies in which the leader is the inventor more innovative?
One recent and interesting article[51] reveals that inventor-led companies produced more patents and that these patents were more commercial and influential than patents awarded to non-inventor-led firms. Also, innovations related to those patents have a greater chance of producing breakthrough products. It seems that leaders that have experience in creating innovations will also have more chances to

---

51 Harvard Business Review: Research: Companies Led by Inventors Produce Better Innovations by Emdad Islam and Iason Zein. https://hbr.org/2019/09/research-companies-led-by-inventors-produce-better-innovations.

create innovation systems in their companies as they have their own insights into the creative process. That means that they could better understand development teams, have better tolerance for failures and be a magnet for other innovators to join or stay in the company. They could also be more passionate in following the company's vision and – what is maybe most important – their employees will listen and follow them in their vision.

11 Introverts as the Majority?

Originality thrives in seclusion free of outside influences beating upon us to cripple the creative mind. Be alone – that is the secret of invention: be alone, that is when ideas are born.
– Nikola Tesla

Making introverts successful innovators

I have two sons and they are so different. They have the same interests, but comparing their social skills or the way they communicate, they are totally different. Since they were three years old and started Kindergarten, we knew for sure that one is an introvert and other is an extrovert. You know, they both talk, yell and scream at home, but in public one still can't stop talking and the other doesn't speak at all. I know why; I'm also an introvert.

A few years ago, I was at a school meeting where a school psychologist gave us a lecture about kids at the age of 8 or 9 years and the pressure they feel in school. It was a good analysis of many groups of behaviours among kids, but I missed some words about introverts. They are not recognised and not all teachers know how to handle them. This goes beyond education – it extends to companies as well.

We know that half of the population are introverts, but mainly our educational, organisational and company systems are oriented toward extroverts. In some environments, introverts are a huge majority (e.g., in software development companies) and we have a problem reaching these people and getting them involved in innovation activities.

We are working with people who sit at the back of the brainstorming workshop and don't say a word. No matter how interesting and the inspiring the session could be, they will not join the conversation. Some of them are closed in their own world and have no intention of sharing their ideas. These people could have the next big thing, too! The question is how to make them idea-submitters?

Adapt.

Make the innovation process closer to them in order to attract them. First, forget about brainstorming. I have seen many times that introverts are sitting somewhere at the back of the room, trying to not make a sound, and then someone else gets loud and they just let them go on.

The ideation process must be closer to everyone and this can be accomplished by introducing challenges run with online tools. This should allow them to have enough time and space to elaborate on their ideas. And they will do that without verbal communication, at least without the need to speak in front of a group. And they should be allowed to do it that way.

https://doi.org/10.1515/9783110654448-011

Outside companies, we can see people who see open idea challenges but just read and never get involved. There are also people who read of crowdfunding projects but are too shy to start their own, or who read about entrepreneurial projects, but never start one. This is the point to go back to educational systems which must be adapted to give introverts better chances or some courage for the future.

Carl Jung coined the terms "introvert" and "extrovert" in the early 1920s.[52]

Introversion. A mode of psychological orientation where the movement of energy is toward the inner world.

A few interesting things about introverts:
- Sometimes they use extra energy just to be "invisible"
- They process internally [53]
- They enjoy being alone and need alone time
- They hate small-talk
- Introverts are 50% of the population

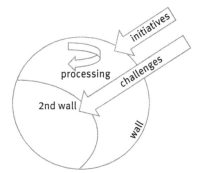

Figure 11.1: Walls around introverts.

This illustration (Figure 11.1) is an attempt at explaining two walls (or psychological barriers) around introverts. The first is broken if you intrigue them enough with an innovation initiative. They will think about the task, but still don't make the necessary effort to be active. Still, there is another wall, as they have to take action in order to post an idea or approach the responsible person. The second wall is broken by making their lives easier with a challenge that requires only a short explanation of the idea by mail or using a submission form. Any kind of written communication is bringing them closer to process, as opposed to brainstorming or design thinking workshops. In short, the way to break both walls is a kind of innovation challenge.

---

52 Beth Buelow: Introvert Entrepreneur, Virgin Books (12 Nov. 2015).
53 Beth Buelow: Introvert Entrepreneur, Virgin Books (12 Nov. 2015).

Introverts can also be engaged in the conversation about open innovation issues, using a kind of social media on an innovation platform. Using comments or discussion in a tool that supports the innovation process can awaken the spirit of collaboration and bring new ideas to the innovation project. Such a method could not only make innovators more open to the outside but also bring new people into the process. This tool could also make life easier for innovation managers when they need to profile innovators (and commenters) and add them into groups (experts or just people interested in a topic).

After recognising innovators, they could be asked to write corporate blogs or wikis as a way of expressing themselves. In the end, introverts could be recognised as innovators or collaborators and express their urge to be creative or collaborate in interesting innovative projects.

Next is an example how a big IT company created an innovation portal with a social-media style collaboration that acts as a starting point for innovation challenges and a platform for further engagement.

Example: Cisco's innovation hub

Cisco's Innovation Hub,[54] is a go-to portal for all things innovation. In 2015, Cisco committed to infusing a culture of innovation across its enterprise through a company-wide effort that became known as "My Innovation". One of the cornerstones of "My Innovation" is a company-wide competition for a new product, process, or service ideas known as the Innovate Everywhere Challenge (IEC). Employee feedback after the challenge noted several common suggestions:
- Employees didn't know where they could share and develop their new ideas outside of the IEC.
- Many employees were surprised to learn about other innovation programmes and events across the organisation and wanted to be able to find these more easily.
- Employees were hungry for ways to connect to others within the organisation who shared their passions and could discuss or mentor them.

A new portal had to allow employees to actively engage in innovation activities and not just consume innovation resources. The portal was made before the second IEC, which would drive thousands of Cisco employees to the Innovation Hub and quickly seed a significant volume of engagement and activity.

Soon after introducing the Innovation Hub, the development team started to add features that made it a wider innovation platform.

---

54 Whitepaper: Cisco's Innovation Hub, 2018.

The team quickly built several new features:
- user profiles for employees with their expertise, business interests and passions
- the ability for employees to invest free tokens in others' ideas and give feedback to idea submitters

Enabling employees to create their own teams on the Innovation Hub has improved the quality of submissions to the innovation challenges. People interested in submitting an entry now put out calls asking, for example, "Who else is passionate about virtual reality and has a marketing background?"

By early 2017, 14,000 employees were already using the Innovation Hub. The next thing were design-thinking principles which were put into practice by the Hub team. It conducted multiple rounds of user feedback, focusing on "extreme users" – those whose data indicated were top contributors and users of the Innovation Hub. Also, things from social networks such as personalised "feed" of news related to innovation and a "Mark Your Calendar" view. Also, a "Discover and Engage" menu was added where users could find all existing Cisco innovation challenges, programmes, events and spaces.

Finally, the Hub team made an opportunity for all employees to create their own events, programmes, and spaces and invited others to participate, which fostered deeper and more extended engagement on the Innovation Hub.

With so much of the friction involved in managing an innovation challenge removed, the number of innovation challenges across Cisco increased along with participation in longstanding challenges. The number of innovation challenges held across Cisco went from three in fiscal year 2017 to 20 in fiscal year 2018. In FY2018, more than 40,000 employees – about 56% of Cisco's total workforce – visited the Innovation Hub.

As of 2018, the most popular functionalities on the Innovation Hub were:
- searching for mentors,
- looking for challenges and events,
- participating in challenges and
- commenting in discussion groups on specific ventures.

Several indicators suggest that the portal is accelerating innovation at Cisco:
- The number of mentors has increased (4,000, up from 2,706 in 2017).
- The number of innovation challenges hosted on the Innovation Hub increased from three to 20 in one year, thanks to the ease and convenience of creating and hosting a challenge.
- The number of events posted on the Innovation Hub jumped from 60 to 200 in one year.

–   Employees stated that the Innovation Hub has added visibility to the range of innovation opportunities and resources across the company, which has led to increased engagement.

The next thing being planned is to gamify the platform to recognise users based on their level of participation and contribution to innovation and also to give users suggestions on how they can become better innovators.

12 Inspire Developers

You might not think that programmers are artists, but programming is an extremely creative pro-
fession. It's logic-based creativity.   *– John Romero*

There are a bunch of questions coming from developers in companies where innovation is not ignited, such as:

Is my task to innovate? I'm here to do my tasks only. Where is the funding?
How will my idea be supported? How can I find the time to think about anything
except my current tasks?

Building innovation culture is surely an important task, but in a software development environment is it also important to inspire future innovators – developers.

How to convince a developer to write down an idea?

Developers are creative beings, they find new solutions on a daily basis; so they
somehow have to be creative, right? Yes, but ...

I was very disappointed to discover that they are often very reluctant to submit
or explain their ideas.

There are two reasons for this:
1. They don't trust others, or they think others will spoil their ideas. Maybe others
    will not understand it or maybe they will not know how to realise them.
2. They want to code and finish it before anyone knows about it. The idea is their
    baby and no one should know about it before the first stable version.

So, I was often seeing developers submitting incremental ideas, which generate
savings or they have small improvements to their current product, but they will not
do it if they don't see the benefit. A small presentation in front of their colleagues or
bosses was often enough to praise them. Also, as already mentioned, rewards will
also help in triggering idea submission.

But what about business ideas? For providing "big" or business ideas, they really
must trust the company. If they are disappointed or have no belief in the innovation
process of the company, you can forget assuring them that their potential ideas have
a chance for realisation. Related to this, it can be said that there are **three types of
programmers** according to their belief in innovation inside the company:
1. **Improvers** – They are creating small tools or scripts, which will help them or
    their team in setting up the environment or in easier and faster testing or auto-
    mation. These are improvements for everyday work, which can help a team by
    saving time and, in the end, money. Often, these tools just stay on their ma-
    chines or sometimes they are shared with the team, but tools are almost never

https://doi.org/10.1515/9783110654448-012

shared within the whole company if there is no improvement management as part of the innovation process.

2. **Non-believers** – There is no chance to get an idea from this kind of developer, as they have no belief in the system. The only hope for getting ideas is in having a presentation of success stories, but the outcome is – even then – uncertain. In the case of experienced developers, it is much more difficult than with younger ones, as they may have some historical difficulties with their superiors or the whole company. Sometimes they are frustrated with their job or their role in the team. In that case, again the best weapon to use is success stories that will show them that their colleagues were able to get their ideas processed and developed into products or improvements. Also, innovation can sometimes help in praising the work of some individuals who do not stand out in other fields of work. Involvement in innovation activities could be a part of a yearly or quarterly talk between the employee and his or her direct superior and may ignite action among some non-believers, but this must not be mandatory.

3. **Innovators** – They are always innovative and even if their previous ideas could not be realised, these persons will always generate new ideas. This kind of developer must be recognised and "nurtured" inside the company. They are often part of "task force teams" or "VIP teams" which are used in special calls for ideas or targeted brainstorming sessions. It is also very beneficial to put many innovators together in a room with a hot topic and a facilitator who has the lead role, separating discussion and generated ideas from unnecessary dead ends.

In the end, those brilliant people will generate ideas; the only thing left is **making them visible** (both ideas and developers). Also, they could be a part of experts, trend hunters of trend spotters groups gathered under a technology management initiative in the company.

> *I have no special talents. I am only passionately curious.* — *Albert Einstein*

Triggers for product innovation

Product development in software companies is structured in a serious and often demanding process that includes customer and market analysis on the one side and agile product development in a software development environment on the other. Simply put, new ideas for new features of products are often coming from a customer or from the market.

But the product development process can be turned around and started from the top with the question: "How can we make a new or better product?"

Answers to that question are new questions, such as: Which new features are needed? How to evolve our product? Again, knowledge of market needs, listening to customers and keeping an eye on technology evolution is the way to move forward, as shown on the third level in the Figure 12.1. The bottom of the diagram shows that taking customer surveys and doing the market analysis is a way to get the information needed for the next iteration of the product development process. Watching technology and then adopting needed technologies are surely most important in an industry that is evolving so fast and also important for any product innovation. This brings us to the last need: new skills. Developers and all other parties involved in product development must be able to take further steps in education to be able to keep track of all necessary changes that the future brings.

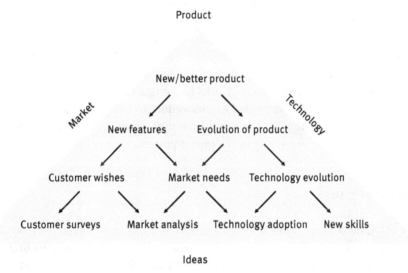

Figure 12.1: Product innovation in software companies.

This pyramid also shows how to ignite product innovation by starting with a simple question at the top and broadening it to the questions at the bottom.

"Easy Innovation" – direct connection with an idea

The easiest ideas are those that come from an innovator's "working space", her everyday work, her tasks and goals, and her expertise. Ideas like new scripts for setting up an environment, or tools for log tracking and error finding – which surely already exist, but are not recognised or are in the planning for the near future – could stimulate new ideas. Hence, these ideas need some kind of recognition and a place in the innovation programme. They can be called incremental innovation or improvements, but what is important is to treat them like "real" innovations. And there are a lot of such ideas in every development environment. Every team certainly has a few ideas and after recognising them, this could trigger new thinking. Ideas from a person's own working space are the easiest not just to ideate, but also to evaluate. This could be done in a straightforward way – quickly and done by a direct superior.

I saw departments with no innovation before Awareness Workshop, but with more than 10 already implemented (but not recognised) ideas after it.

Other chances for a kind of "easy innovation" are those ideas that are born in contact with the customer. In some cases, the customer may complain about some current features and then the other side can think about some new ideas as the answer to those complaints for a future version of the product. These ideas must also be considered as innovation and this can bring to life an innovation culture in companies that maybe think about themselves having no innovation at all. Such classification should not be misused, but it has to be taken as the start of the innovation movement, which must bring new changes to the product and the company.

The only case when there is no innovation born in the contact with the customer is when the customer literally asks for certain changes. This is a normal, everyday job and must not be treated as innovation, but as a customer request. I had the task of distinguishing such features from innovations and it was not easy without knowing the whole product development process.

Beginner's look

One of the most popular methods of ideation is looking at the problem from a different angle or another perspective. At least this is the most favourite technique for me. Inside the company, this is often difficult and should be done in an isolated environment using a special method and a skilled moderator, as it is not easy to move away from prejudices. Then new questions and later new ideas can arise which could shed new light on the topic. A beginner's look is a valuable method to get to new ideas, but it is often difficult to initiate in environments where the same products have existed for years. One way is to involve people who are working "on the edge of the project" and are not deeply involved and to use them, as they might more easily step back from the current offerings and bring a fresh perspective.

Gamification

Gamification could be a great way to inspire developers and other persons involved in the software development process and it could be done using cards or boards. This could move the point of view to different places and give a new perspective to innovators. As everyone knows, gaming is so close to software engineers and any kind of game brings a smile to their faces no matter how old they are. The younger generation of developers were born and raised in the era of video games and most of them played (or are still playing) games for hours every day. That caused that they think and act differently and this could be a great asset for their creativity and adaptability in daily work. Gaming teaches everyone about learning from failures through iterative attempts to finish some mission or in-game task. Also, gaming teaches about learning on the fly as you don't have to know everything before starting a game (project) and you will learn everything playing the game (work).

In the case of software engineers, board games can work – but only if the game could be done on a screen which will bring new ideas for current and future products? Maybe the first step towards creativity in an IT organisation could be to make some kind of innovation game?

Gamification could be done as a way of open innovation. A famous example is IBM's CityOne from the year 2010, which was designed to help IBM's industry and business clients easily understand the potential effect of smart city solutions in areas of energy, water, retail and banking.[55]Something similar could be offered to the world or to a closed group like experts, all employees, partners, customers or a student group in order to ignite creativity in a certain area of business.

It is always a struggle to get most of the people when practicing innovation as there is always a group of innovators, but that's often not enough. One way of igniting developers to innovate and disrupt everyday routines is organising internal hackathons. This is an effective way to catch their interest. The example comes from Dropbox, where they organise an annual Hack Week for everyone in the company who come together to "experiment with new ideas and ways of working".[56]

Mixed teams

Experts from another domain can be used to increase chances of having a fresh look at the problem or topic. If possible, even mixed teams could be formed which is usually the way to create interesting and successful idea generation, but also other stages of the idea journey. Technical people often lack customer and business perspective and they are putting solutions at the front without seeing a wider picture. On the other hand, proposals coming from business-oriented people are harder to action.[57]

For example, in design sprints a team is formed by the decider (maybe the CEO), a finance expert, marketing expert, customer expert, tech or logistics expert and a design expert.

55 http://www.gamesforcities.com/database/cityone-a-smarter-planet-game/.
56 Hack Week, Dropbox. https://www.dropbox.com/blackops/projects/hack-week.
57 Susana Jurado Apruzzese, Maria Olano Mata: Lean Elephants – Addressing the Innovation Challenge in Big Companies, Innovation and Research – Telefonica I+D, 2014.

Experts

In every company, there are people who are masters in their own field. They know in detail everything about their product and are highly valuable to their environment. But what about innovation? Can you expect innovation from experts?

If they are closed inside the walls of the company and inside the knowledge areas where they are so good, then the only ideas that can occur are incremental. To be able to produce radical ideas, experts must be open to other fields of work, new technologies that go beyond just new versions of their product or similar. Experts can be valuable but must be "integrated" into an innovation programme.

Experts are often recognised by making a special "experts programme" or simply by giving them a "senior" sign before their working title. This rewards their knowledge, but in an innovation programme everyone is equal, there is no "seniority" there. So, experts should not only be carefully integrated but also carefully "managed" inside the system. I will get back to this topic in the chapter "Technology Management".

An additional step in the right direction is creating internal training centres where people could attend lectures, which should inspire and provide knowledge on necessary topics, which can be directly related to work, but also be a part of a personal development programme.

Reach the full potential

Everyone wants to be fulfilled and to reach happiness through the fulfilment of personal goals. Can this be done in companies?

Psychologist Abraham Maslow proposed the theory known as Maslow's hierarchy of needs as shown in Figure 12.2.

It is portrayed in the shape of a pyramid with the most fundamental needs at the bottom, as the most basic needs, which must be achieved before people get motivated to achieve higher-level needs.

Let's bring this to the workspace of software companies. Physiological needs at the bottom of the pyramid portray universal human needs and can be labelled as the ability to work in the company's workspace. Together with the next layer, safety, these constitute "basic needs". In the safety layer are the company's benefits and security (financial, health). The next two layers together are called psychological needs, where belonging and love in the workspace are replaced by a sense of acceptance in a workgroup and the connection with colleagues.[58] Esteem could mean the feeling of respect

---

58 Langdon Morris, Moses Ma, Po Chi Wu: Agile Innovation: The Revolutionary Approach to Accelerate Success, Inspire Engagement, and Ignite Creativity, John Wiley & Sons (7 Nov. 2014).

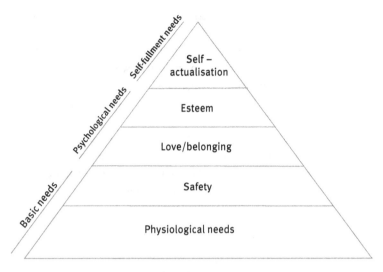

Figure 12.2: Maslow's hierarchy of needs.

from others, status in the company and recognition. Together, these all influence productivity in the team or organisation.

At the top of the pyramid is self-actualization, which means reaching the full potential of the individual. Maslow describes this as the desire to accomplish everything that one can, to become the most that one can be. In companies, this could be strongly connected with innovation, as this fulfilling of full potential could be done developing the abilities and talents of individuals which results in creativity and, in the end, innovation. This is the reason why innovators are intrinsically motivated and when their ideas are realised, they feel joy in the company, become loyal, and fulfilled.

Make it mandatory?

Collaboration and involvement in innovation activities must be voluntary. I saw an example where one middle manager made innovation a mandatory activity in his business unit. In yearly check-ups – a kind of manager-employee meeting about performance and the future of every person – one of the mandatory questions was: How many innovation proposals did you have in the last year?

Of course, this was counterproductive, what I as innovation manager strongly felt. This business unit had the poorest results despite this mandatory participation in an innovation programme. The innovation climate was going down and the simplest reason was this forcing of innovation.

People simply didn't feel good because of this obligation. Some were coming to me to get help on how to submit "anything", others would submit one idea and then drop any thoughts about innovation for a year. Some sent a few ideas but were reluctant to participate in other activities.

Simply, this is not a way to do it. The innovator must have freedom without constraints and some people (somewhere it is a majority) will never participate; there is no need to force them. In addition, if people are currently busy or simply focused on their tasks, it is not wise to force them to submit ideas, as this will destroy all future chances.

Now, I will add three examples. The first one is the example of product innovation triggered by market and technology evolution. The next example is describing the innovation ecosystem in a big IT company. The last example is describing the setup of an innovation network whose members act as ambassadors across the company.

Example: Enea Data Manager – product innovation

Enea develops network software for the connected society and provides solutions for mobile traffic optimization, subscriber data management, network virtualisation, traffic classification, embedded operating systems and professional services.

The Enea Policy and Access Control portfolio provides innovative software-based functions for the control plane in telecom networks. The main functional areas supported by the portfolio are access control (AAA) through Enea Access Manager and policy control (PCRF) through Enea Policy Manager.

After 10+ years of providing AAA and PCRF installations on many customer sites around the world, there was an opportunity for new product development during a time of rapid changes to the market with the introduction of 5G. It was inevitable for AAA and PCRF products to evolve, but now the challenge was to include a new network element in the portfolio. This element – Unified Data Management (UDM) was developed after a quick reaction to market demand.

It can be said that product management was triggered from the market side, but also the technology side (5G) by studying market and standardisation. Product management decided to cover a new key domain and UDM was a missing piece. Also, the tiered 5G architecture defined UDM more precisely which supported the decision to launch the project. The reaction was quick, R&D was excited about broadening the portfolio and very fast and effective in analysing the area. The product was made by prioritising this task and (as always) using an agile process. The launched product, the Enea Data Manager, was on the market in time and customer reactions confirmed that this product was the right decision.

Several years ago, a similar story occurred with PCRF (Enea Policy Manager), the project that was recognised as innovation and was partially funded through an innovation programme that supported the development of a new product.

Example: Ericsson Nikola Tesla – innovation ecosystem

Ericsson Nikola Tesla is an associated company of the Ericsson Group that operates in the global ICT market. The company's activities include marketing and sales, research and development, design of total communication solutions, and services in the multi-service and mobile networks area, including mobile internet and complex system integration in all business areas. The company also provides innovative solutions in health care, transport, state administration, municipal services and multimedia that constantly improve people's lives and create new value.

Ericsson Nikola Tesla has reached a size of around 3,000 people, among which are about 1,500 developers working in research and development.

They differentiate between incremental ideas, disruptive ideas (a process which requires newly formed teams), and patents as the ultimate outcome of the innovation process. Organising events (hackathons, innovation days) is equally important for the maintenance of an innovation culture.

The company has a network of innovation managers that is complemented by innovation experts who are used in the idea evaluation process. The process is supported by a company-wide tool where anyone can submit an idea at any point in time from whatever field – even outside of the company's portfolio.

Additionally, innovation challenges are defined by top management or in some cases by middle management. Idea generation in a challenge is usually done within a single month, followed by a period of evaluation and implementation. Implementation is mainly done by the business unit which defined the topic for the challenge at the start, but not always. Sometimes ideas that are recognised as good ideas, but are beyond the scope of the unit's work, are taken over by another department or (in some cases) by innovation management at the company's headquarters.

Concerning products, priority is given to ideas connected with market requirements, but also some ideas for new features of products are coming through open tools (innovation process). The product manager makes a decision about the features for new release.

The development of solutions is done using agile/scrum/kanban methodology and through retrospectives, putting the focus on innovations by making features for new sprints (as improvements); this could not even be done through the tool.

Innovators are recognised in a way that direct superior knows who is active in the team.

Rewards are defined by the company rulebook (bottom-up ideas). Special prizes are available for innovation challenges where the best idea (or best 3) get a reward and are also presented to leadership teams. Another way of innovation recognition is an innovation wall with the best ideas in recent years.

Looking to the future, in a short-term period the focus should be on cooperation with other companies, particularly on the topic of 5G where many new application possibilities are possible in the fields of technology, industry, cities and other sectors.

Example: Worldline – WIN innovators group

WIN, which stands for "Worldline Innovation Network", is the umbrella under which Worldline organises the promotion, facilitation and development of innovation. Created in 2005, the network is spread throughout the company (from both geographic and organisational viewpoints). It is animated by WIN Members who act as innovation ambassadors, facilitators and promoters and have very diverse profiles. They are chosen according to three main criteria: their interest in innovation, their geographic and organisational influence and endorsement from their management. WIN activities are structured into three tracks.

The first track focuses on the cultural aspect, i.e., innovative mindset and basic skills, such as creativity, idea-friendliness, openness, etc. It's the preparation of the soil.

The second track aims at stimulating innovation and creating conditions for new ideas to sparkle, for example, through calls for ideas, thought-provoking content sharing, interactions with external entities, or cross-silo events. It's the fertilization.

The third track addresses the innovation process for the purpose of collecting innovative ideas and turning them into concrete innovations. It's the cultivation.

13 Environmental Effects

Creativity training in different environments

Creativity is a great motivator because it makes people interested in what they are doing. Creativity gives hope that there can be a worthwhile idea. Creativity gives the possibility of some sort of achievement to everyone. Creativity makes life more fun and more interesting.

– Edward de Bono

There are many different environments or ecosystems inside IT companies, like product development teams, testing – people responsible for automation, platform-related issues solvers, product release teams, salespersons or customer support teams. Let's see now how to approach these different groups of people existing in IT companies.

Different teams need different forms of training from the start. So, the next question must be: How do you trigger innovation in environments that rely on safe bets driven by the market?

Before developing the training, the facilitator must know the environment. Are there some known innovators from the past here? Have we had any ideas from this team in the last few years? Are they active in innovation challenges? Has this team any time to stop, think and listen? If not, why even bother them with creativity training?

In an environment where there is no time for anything other than solving problems or errors, dedicated time for innovation can help and a few hours weekly or monthly can open up some pathways to ideas.

One study showed that 31 hours/month are spent on average by employees in unproductive meetings,[59] so maybe this is the first point to look at in order to find time for ideas? Organising time may be the first innovation challenge in some departments. Making improvements to save time should be the first task, the starting point of innovation efforts; this could open the door for further success.

After getting the team to an innovation workshop (awareness workshop) as the first part of the initiative, the opportunity must not be wasted and they should take part in deciding what's next. Maybe the team is predetermined only for improvements? However, any agenda must be able to be quickly adapted. Of course, trainings should be separated by groups of participants related to their needs.

The first group of training participants is technicians who are strongly tied to their everyday job and are more open to improvements. They will always be looking for ways to make things better, faster and more efficient.

Next are those developers that have broad interests (hopefully, a majority of them). Some are strictly connected with their next tasks and products, but a large part is always open to future scenarios, market trends or simply to innovation (of course, there is a part of the first group – technicians – who could fit here).

---

59 http://www.atlassian.com/time-wasting-at-work-infographic.

https://doi.org/10.1515/9783110654448-013

Product leaders, by default, must be open to market trends and look out for the future of their business. Their job is to be innovative, but most have a problem with it and that surely makes them the first candidates for creative training.

Salespersons should change their perspective and try to add their thoughts about the future of the whole company, knowing its current position in the market. They have a great starting point for creativity, but do they exploit it? In my experience, most do not. Customer innovation workshops could be a place where they could share their ideas.

Executives could be innovators, but sometimes it may be enough from their side to support the creative process.

The creative approach is different for all of the groups mentioned; some need market and trends insights, others just a reality check – what can be done in their organisation and what is simply not possible.

Regional environment and innovation

> In fact, most people are being squeezed in their little cubicle, and their creativity is forced out elsewhere, because the company can't use it. The company is organized to get rid of variants.
> – Scott Adams

How to put your company in a bubble (its own ecosystem) and not let external events to affect you and your climate?

Innovative companies sometimes must be isolated to be successful. Not every regional environment is positive, and not all cities and countries have a good atmosphere for entrepreneurs, startups or even companies. Then it's necessary to isolate.

The company can really create its own bubble where everyone will feel positive and inspired, no matter what happens outside, just in front of the office windows. Sometimes this is the only way to prosper as some cities or countries don't have the right entrepreneurship or innovation climate.

Education systems, migration or even political turbulence affect the business climate. But there are examples of prosperous and innovative startups or companies from every place in the world. They made it because of isolation from the outside.

I have an example of igniting an innovation culture in a company that had three locations in three parts of the country. Each of these towns has its own culture and this was strongly reflected in all innovation efforts. Every location, every team must be carefully accessed and then there is a chance for innovation to flourish.

Big companies can have dedicated innovation managers for every business unit, for every city or country. Often the best way to reach everyone in the company is to have a dedicated expert who can communicate in their own language and translate all supporting documentation into the local language; this helps even when everyone in the company speaks English.

Locations

Figure 13.1 shows the number of ideas in five innovation challenges. It is interesting to see it sliced into three locations – three cities. It is clear that ideas are not distributed evenly as the second city has the most ideas, while the third city has the least.

Results can't be ideal and there is no way to have a perfectly even distribution, but here is a case where the pattern is repeated five times. I must say that City 2 had the strongest innovation culture and the biggest number of innovators in all challenges and during all innovation activities. Cities 1 and 3 also had experts and innovators, but their innovation culture wasn't on the same level, and it was triggered only during certain innovation challenges, but to a smaller degree than the second city. Other effects were more involvement in innovation workshops and (not related to innovation activities) greater loyalty of employees in the second city.

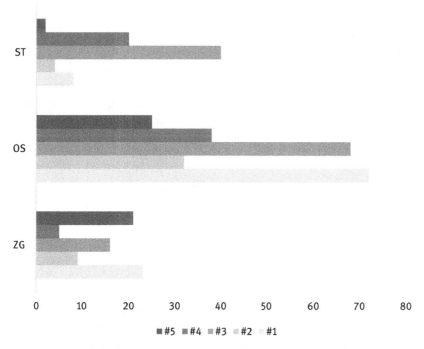

Figure 13.1: Comparison of the number of ideas during five innovation challenges in three locations.

The culture was affected by local measures, but also by external stimuli, such as more fluctuation and competition in the job market in City 3, and by smaller, isolated teams in City 1. Maybe the fluctuation in City 3 is the consequence of a lacking innovation culture?

Work environment

Everyone wants to work in a high-tech office where you can feel nice and comfortable. But this must be not only visible but also felt. Office design, office culture, and innovation culture must be linked in a successful environment. Light, noise or heat can influence productivity, but also ideation. There are cases when this is not noticed and where software companies don't much care about the office environment. In other cases, the care is focused on making "innovation rooms" with whiteboards and modern furniture or "rooms for fun" with darts or table soccer, but without such care being given to the part of the building where people actually work. Innovation rooms sometimes end up not being used and have a good chance of becoming a kind of company storehouse.

Decorating the workspace and creating spaces where people can meet and talk are not without reason part of activities in many big innovative companies all over the world.

Ideation in external places

It is always a welcome idea to hold brainstorming sessions outside of the company. This moves all participants away from their desks, laptops, meetings, micromanagers and colleagues that will search for them. The facilitator will have a much easier task to motivate and initiate ideation. The place must be carefully selected; it must provide inspiration, but not distract. Something completely different from the office sounds great!

It is difficult to expect that people who work 7, 8 or 10 hours in the office to be creative in that same place; the idea of taking them outside could bring results and should be considered.

Innovation flow

When I was thirteen and in seventh grade, my German teacher asked me to speak about a topic completely in German. I hadn't studied much for it, but I tried to make something with what I knew from the past. I started talking and sentences were coming out, one after another with pretty much no mistakes. I was using my vocabulary perfectly, everything was flowing through me and the result was remarkable for me. I got an excellent grade and later that day I was asking myself why was I so good? Simply put, I entered the zone.

Innovation flow – the zone or something similar – is the special state when your ideas are coming to you in a series and your mind is roaming free. Everyone has experienced it, but can it be induced?

The Zone[60]– when all the senses are sharpened and the focus is on what is being done. No feeling for external or what's around.   – Davor Rostuhar

How to come into flow or the "zone"?
This is a hard question as everyone is different and this psychological state occurs at different times for each person. It can come during cycling, running in the countryside or in the park, walking and thinking, daydreaming, traveling and watching how other people live, while reading a book …

Do you see what is common for these activities?

None of them is happening in the workplace! Yes, people get their ideas mostly outside the office. The thing companies can do about this is to adapt and make innovation activities that will support time outside the office. Innovation challenges are one way to do it.

How to make an environment for it?
Everyone will say that many ideas are born in the shower. The reason is that this place is without distractions and it gives a relaxing feeling. The shower effect should be replicated in order to get ideas in challenges. So, it is necessary to feel safe and to have the needed time to shape an idea. Maybe this can only be done in the safest environment – the innovator's home.

In one survey, 72% of the people said that they experienced new ideas in the shower.[61] Even CEOs said in one study [62] that they came up on only 19% of their best ideas in the office, while 17% had them in the car, 15% in the shower, 11% on vacation, and 8% in the gym. Ideas are born outside of the office, so try to exploit that.

Even when the idea is born outside the office, it will be submitted to the innovation platform in the office. This is the time when it will be written and re-shaped for the first time.

The problem with open offices

I'm sure most people hate open offices; I hate them too. But companies are still using them and this will not change anytime soon. After cubicles, open offices are the environment most software developers must feel to be normal, but is it an inspirational and creative environment?

---

60 Davor Rostuhar: Polarni San, prva hrvatska ekspedicija na južni pol, KEK 2018.

61 Survey contributed to by cognitive psychologist Scott Barry Kaufman, Ph.D., and commissioned by Hansgrohe. https://www.pmmag.com/articles/96968-hansgrohe-study-the-brightest-ideas-begin -in-the-shower.

62 2014 INC. 500 2014 CEO Survey https://www.inc.com/magazine/201409/inc.500-2014-inc-500-ceo-survey-results.html.

They were invented as a place for bringing people together in order to collaborate, make new ideas happen and foster creativity across teams. But is this true?

If you ask developers, many will say they would love to have a day or two during the week when they can work from home so they can get some tasks done faster; they can't work in an open office because of frequent distractions. Noise, movements and other distractions make open offices places where it is hard to focus, hard to work, and hard to innovate.

Many will say that new ideas can't be born in such an atmosphere, but for most managers, the only option is to adapt and bring in innovation efforts that will live in such conditions. As agile work scenarios must live in open offices, the same goes for innovation scenarios. Adaptation will mean putting all activities online and in the case of innovation teams – to isolate them in some (quiet) corner of the office.

The problem with home offices

Many developers today work from home a few days a week or full-time. It is surely helpful to work in a comfortable environment such as a home office, but isolation from the company office can also de-stimulate. There is no easy answer to how the home office affects a person concerning creativity and innovation, and it is dependent on the individual. The company, again, must adapt its innovation efforts by considering this.

Again, innovation challenges may be the answer to the problems related to open offices.

14 Innovation Challenges

> Coming up with an idea is the least important part of creating something great. It has to be the right idea and have good taste, but the execution and delivery are what's key.   – Sergey Brin

In my humble opinion, the best way for quick and simple idea generation inside organisations are innovation challenges. This is the way to solve the introvert problem (break the psychological barrier when submitting ideas), but also to connect customer and market knowledge with all participants. It could also connect recent and existing knowledge of technology trends. Of course, innovation challenges must be carefully prepared in order to be successful.

Now, I will add the example of a "call for ideas" that I used in my former company. After many attempts with innovation workshops and brainstorming sessions, we needed something that could be done in a fast and efficient way – even remotely.

I tried to develop a tool for quick and fast gathering of ideas in a software development ecosystem of around 300 developers in three towns, doing everything remotely with mails and telcos. I found this to be a quick and easy way to ignite innovation in the organisation.

Figure 14.1: Call for ideas – wide challenge for everyone in the company.

https://doi.org/10.1515/9783110654448-014

I must point out that the topic was not focused, but open to anything that could be part of the company's future.

Here is a small guideline on how to do it:

First step: The call

Whether the company has a size of 15, 150 or 1,500 people, the easiest way (and politest as we saw in the chapter "Introverts as the Majority") to reach everyone is email.

The focus group can include everyone – as a sort of internal open innovation, or a selected group like former innovators (if tracked in the past), tech gurus, newcomers or product specialists. It is selected using data from former initiatives (for innovators) or using technology management data (for experts).

The mail should come from the CEO or sales manager who invites colleagues to participate in the call in order to introduce a new topic to the company's portfolio or new features for the next generation of existing products. It should be a short mail with the invitation, deadline and most importantly – a brief explanation of the topic or problem (as shown in Figure 14.1). It is very important to be short but to the point; everyone must understand the task and be motivated to join the challenge.

Two-week period for idea generation

The deadline should be 10–15 days in order to not lose focus, but people still should have enough time to come up with thoughts on the topic over one or two weekends or several drives home or a few daydreaming times when ideas could arise. Ideas are here deliberately targeted to be ignited outside the office. Let's say this in a developers' way: we launch a background process which will ensure that people think about the call when they are relaxed and ready for ideation.

Site with all ideas

The next task is to have all the ideas in one place. Everyone should have the option to read already submitted ideas and to build on them or be inspired by them. A web-based application, shared table or even SharePoint site will do the job. If there is idea management software in use, that's the best choice, of course.

Along with the name of each submitter and a short description (not details), this list should also have the current state of the ideas. Later, the state of ideas should be appropriately changed in order to make the process transparent. Having this list visible to all should trigger new ideas and make the process reliable and accessible for everyone. It should also trigger the innovation manager about the state of the initiative and the need for further reminder emails, news, or new triggers during the ideation phase.

Presentation to stakeholders

After the deadline, when all ideas are available and listed, the facilitator must prepare a presentation to stakeholders (management, sales and experts). In my example, this presentation was done in the form of one slide = one idea, as the ideas must be explained briefly without wasting much time. All content comes from the innovators who must give a short description of the idea with its key features; this step includes little detail and no technicalities. Any picture, graphics or diagrams are more than welcome, as they will shorten the time needed to explain the essence of the idea. If there is enough time and someone can put the effort in, a prototype can be made, as it will better show the usability than a single slide.

Selection

All stakeholders have a vote on every idea and a chance to directly push some ideas if they find them intriguing. Ideas can have the status "proceed", "closed" or "proceed with explanation". The latter means that ideas may be processed, but only after answering a few questions. Here, the focus is on the question: Can our company develop such an idea in the near future? Closed ideas must be carefully dropped with an explanation which should ensure that these innovators come back with new ideas in the next call. The critical part here is done by the innovation manager or whoever manages the challenge.

Presentation of best ideas

New presentation (again one slide = one idea) should now focus on the question: Do we have a sales channel, market and technology for a business case here? Slides from the first presentation much be enhanced now in order to answer these questions. This is the time when innovators can present their ideas in the form of an elevator pitch or something similar, as this step is also done very quickly – let's say five ideas in five minutes.

Decision

Stakeholders must agree on a decision and the selected idea(s) must have the budget to be processed in the short term. This must come from the CEO or product sponsor who has the time and budget to support the whole challenge and project(s) that are born through it. The prospective idea that becomes a project must have all necessary resources in order to be realised. This has a strong effect on the success of the next call for ideas, as participants are always motivated by the success of previous challenges.

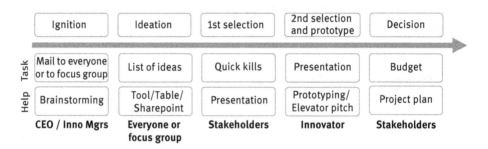

Figure 14.2: Call for ideas.

Side effects of this technique are:
- big number of ideas generated
- quick selection
- suitable for "recruiting" innovators for future campaigns

A crucial part is the availability of resources for implementation, business unit support during all stages and, at the end, sales support during shaping of the challenge.

Next are two examples coming from IT companies. The first example shows how to create an innovation ecosystem with details on the idea management process and innovation culture.

The second shows an example of an idea incubation initiative, a way to support an innovation challenge with the further steps needed for developing innovation.

Such processes should help in establishing fruitful innovation systems in agile organisations, as they support the parallel development process and also teach innovators about intrapreneurship and creative methods.

Example of an innovation system: Lufthansa Systems

Lufthansa Systems[63] is a 100% subsidiary within the Lufthansa group founded in 1995. Today they are one of the world's leading providers of IT services in the airline industry. Their unique strengths come from an ability to combine profound industry know-how with technological expertise and many years of project experience. They have 2,200 employees worldwide.

Prior to 2008, within Lufthansa Systems there was little formal innovation activity – no R&D or innovation department. The main thrust in R&D was done mainly via product development and enhancing existing services and products, or reacting to customer requests.

When the company established the innovation department, the process of managing innovation was done using a stage-gate process. The progress of innovation was dependent on innovation managers who needed to find a department which would perform a review and later actually make innovation happen.

The change in today's innovation system within Lufthansa Systems is that the political element has been removed. When someone comes up with an idea, he or she doesn't need to see a manager; the idea will be brainstormed at creative and design-thinking workshops and it is up to colleagues to decide about its future (as shown in Figure 14.3).

The company realised that their old approach to innovation management also had an impact on employee commitment; employees felt that they could hardly influence the company.

There are two kinds of innovation challenges on which they are focused now. One is with an open kind of question: How can we ensure the future of Lufthansa Systems? This would be the place for asking employees: Do you have any ideas about what we can do? The second type involves closed questions around a technical issue, product, service or any other issue. Experience so far suggests that the open question challenge is not very helpful for a company's innovation performance and the challenges with closed questions seem to be more beneficial.

The first challenge is strategic focus, as a result of portfolio analysis or a technology trend. Ideation should be focused on a topic with the question, How might we?"

To illustrate, Lufthansa Systems would, for instance, post:

> There's a new technology – how can we use that technology within our company to make something, to create value for our customers?" or, "We have that product, and how can we enhance that product?' or 'Here's a customer request, how can we fulfil that customer's request?

---

63 Innovation culture, management, and process at Lufthansa Systems, TACIT Knowledge Alliance, funded by the Erasmus+ Programme of the European Union, Project Number: 562459-EPP-1-2015-1-UK-EPPKA2-KA Project Duration: January 2016 – December 2018.

Lufthansa Systems employees visit the inventIT platform as part of their work and every employee is asked to post an idea. Every employee who works with the platform receives an equivalent of a notional €1,000 for "crowdfunding". With that €1,000, each employee can decide which idea to fund. So, it is no longer the management who decides; it is the trust of colleagues in the idea that matters. For the idea to move forward inside the company, it needs to get 20 votes with at least €50 funding out of a virtual €1,000. It would mean: "That is a cool idea, I believe in it, and we should work on it". If the idea receives 20 votes of confidence (the phase called "sponsoring an idea"), within the forthcoming four weeks a team starts working on it. The first most important issue is the customer value and the answer to the question: Why should we do this?

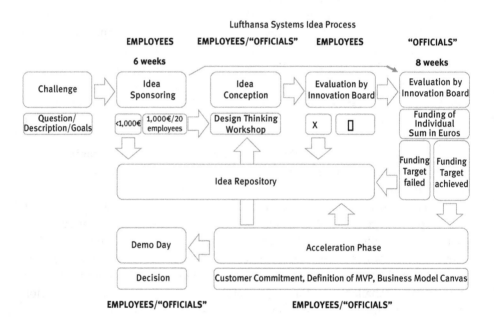

Figure 14.3: Lufthansa Systems' idea process.

The second step in the process is a one-day design-thinking workshop where the team is working on the idea trying to identify a value proposition by asking the questions: Who is the user? What is the pain of the user? What are the next steps in order to make it happen? Colleagues that commented on the idea could also be invited to the workshop. The result of the workshop is a short (2 min.) video, which serves as the innovation pitch for the acceleration phase.

With that video, the innovator(s) takes the idea forward into the funding stage where the short pitch video is published and becomes available to all employees who have the right to vote with the above-mentioned €1,000. Next, employees decide how much to give out of their virtual venturing capital to the now pitching innovation. Once the innovation gets the required virtual amount, the company starts looking into the issues of how soon the required resources can be taken out of the normal operational management and how it could be prototyped.

Next is an "acceleration phase" where the innovators(s) receive up to three months to work on the innovation project. Also, the decision has to be made as to whether a new software development is needed. The idea passes through the issues of customer value and creating the MVP, finding a potential customer and getting the customer's commitment using the support of the innovation department through acceleration labs. The acceleration lab uses design sprint methodology – a 5-day programme to map the problem and identify features and test them, filling out a business model canvas, creating a prototype, inviting externals to test it and, finally, creating a pitch.

On the demo day, managing directors and line managers are required to get together to see three to five pitches which have already passed the acceleration phase. Also, every employee from any location can join demo day and watch the 10-minute presentations done by pitching teams. Demo days are available via link throughout the company so that all employees are able to be a part of innovation pitching.

To make people interested in, and to motivate them to vote, they included a gamified element that involves giving voters points. Depending on how many points an employee gets, he/she can be upgraded from "innovation pioneer" to "innovation master". Another gamification element is around funds. For instance, if one employee funds the idea and on demo day that idea receives the green light to go to the next stage with something like "please go-ahead for full information", then the money that person has put in can be re-used again for different voting.

People start with the €1,000, but then each and every month, they receive €85. So, even if they pledged all of their money after a month, they already have another €85.

Since the introduction of the new system (less than a year ago), almost 40% of the workforce has joined the company's "innovation community" and at least 25% are looking into the tool and working with the tool on a monthly basis.

Innovation culture is more than just a tool for Lufthansa Systems. It is innovative thinking that the company wants to encourage. This type of thinking – *"I'm able to decide which ideas I want to push; I also think about how I can shape and make ideas better"* – is helping to create an innovative culture within Lufthansa Systems.

Example: Worldline's WIN Lift – idea incubation initiative

WIN Lift is Worldline's ideas incubation initiative. It was created to fill the gap between a newborn idea and the expectations of mainstream investment processes in a large company. The design of WIN Lift was notably influenced by Adobe's Kickbox and Eric Ries' Lean Startup. WIN Lift relies on a process structured in three phases. During

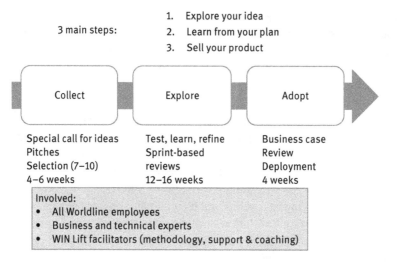

Figure 14.4: WIN Lift.

the first phase (Explore), the innovator is supported by a set of tools, guidelines and some facilitation.

The focus is on giving the newborn idea a chance to take shape and benefit from some early refinement. Objections and judgment are deferred, only questions and suggestions are accepted, until the innovators feels ready to actually present their idea. The second phase (Learn) is focused on actually investigating the idea in an iterative and efficient way. Through a series of sprints, the innovators try to maximise learning – through assumption checking, unknown solving, option testing, etc. – in order to make the idea stronger and collect the necessary data to advocate it. The purpose of the third phase (Sell) is to turn the idea and collected data into a convincing business case and have it adopted by the company: the idea has now reached the mainstream investment process and can live its life. A gate at the end of each phase or iteration of the process decides whether the idea shall iterate, stop or go ahead. WIN Lift operates in two modes: a permanent, open mode, where innovators can submit any idea at any time, and *special calls*, which are more focused in terms of time and scope.

15 Improvements in Development Environment

Excellent firms don't believe in excellence – only in constant improvement and constant change.
– Tom Peters

Improvements are an integral part of the development process, but often they are forgotten and not recognised. It is important to mention that they can trigger bigger ideas and ignite an innovation culture. It is also important to point out that improvements and incremental ideas must be handled differently than radical ideas. The rewarding system, funding, education and approach are much different.

First, improvements are present all over every company, every unit and every team. Software engineers are making improvements to make their life easier. That's how many scripts, small tools, macros or tests are made. A common problem is that these ideas are often forgotten or used by only one person or in the best way by only one team.

To get the most from these ideas it is necessary to first recognise such ideas and later to reward them. As was shown in the chapter "Reward Programme and Effects of Rewarding", it is essential to reward improvements to ensure a constant flow of such ideas.

There are two main types of improvements:
- process and
- product improvements

Process improvements are mostly oriented toward quality (or quality management). Continuous improvements and savings are often part of the quality management processes and are often already in place in many companies. They are a must in big companies, but often there is no trace of them in small or medium organisations. These kind of improvements are not strongly connected to innovation management, so let's put our spotlight on the second type of improvement. I will come back later to process improvement in "Example: innovation challenge for process improvements".

Product improvements or incremental ideas produce savings in the development process or introduce new features (incremental) or small adaptations to known products. These improvements may be funded directly by business units as they could evaluate, get resources for implementation and ultimately realise those ideas.

Continuous improvements process phases should include:
1. preparing the workshop
2. introduction to the workshop
3. understanding the process
4. analyse real state with definition of measure units
5. recording and showing waste

https://doi.org/10.1515/9783110654448-015

6. recording and showing improvements
7. developing solutions for improvements
8. making the catalogue of measures
9. presentation
10. realisation of measures
11. tracking of measures

Transferring this to software development departments or organisations, these steps must be changed in a way to make improvements part of the innovation process in an organisation:
1. prepare the meeting with the team
2. introduction to the workshop
3. recording and showing time which can be saved
4. recording and showing improvements
5. making a list of improvements
6. decision on "GO!" for improvements
7. tracking improvements

After an idea awareness workshop, colleagues are introduced to the system and examples of already existing improvements in the company. The process is introduced and, using examples, the types of expected improvements are now in front of participants. Then, the first ideas are coming to the boards and a list of improvements can be made. Later stages are often as in innovation processes.

When improvements start to be too common and iterative, it is time to change from **passive** to **active** improvement management, which can be done using the next measures with no need for a big investment:
– tracking improvements, their field of effect and their benefit
– giving needed time to idea creators (for realisation of ideas)
– improving the innovation-intrapreneurship culture
– including decision-makers deeper in the innovation (improvement) process
– raising awareness of low and middle management

Rewarding improvements

There can be an easy and transparent way to reward improvements in every environment. First, improvements must have a decision-maker who can evaluate them; this should be someone close to the topic (sometimes it is best that this is the direct superior), but with the allocated budget. Every improvement saves some time, no matter whether it is a process improvement or a tool that will make testing faster. This is essential for evaluation. The benefit is then calculated, as time savings is translated into money savings. The more people that will use the improvement, the greater the benefit. A simplified calculation is done by multiplying the time benefit, hourly cost and the number of people that will use this improvement. Of course, if needed, additional variables can be added to the formula.

Benefit = time savings (yearly) × hourly cost × number of peopleusing improvement

Reward can be a percentage of that benefit multiplied by some other company dependent factors.

Key points

These small incremental innovations (improvements) lead to big savings and make everyday work:
- more efficient,
- faster, and
- eliminate unnecessary costs or waste.

Once more I must point out that improvements are possible everywhere; they just need to be identified. They are a great factor at the start of an innovation programme and can help in raising the level of innovation culture.

In one of my former companies, we had a major success in an improvement programme, indicated by a very high increase in improvement benefit after some years (70% increase in improvement benefit). It was supported in a top-down manner – management was focused on supporting improvements leading to solutions and results in their own department. In addition, bottom-up ideators were instructed to have discussions with their direct superiors in their own departments and were supported by a team of innovation managers.

Example: Innovation challenge for process improvements

Again, my own example of an innovation challenge started to get new process improvements. The target was to improve the effectiveness and efficiency of processes and procedures. The overall goal was to ensure a high standard of project management and delivery quality in our customers' perception.

The company was positioned as a customer-oriented organisation with an excellent quality/price ratio of the services offered. As customer focus was essential, it meant that it was very important how customers perceived the company's project management and the quality of services.

The goal of process descriptions and definitions was to ensure that results were achieved in a planned way and that applying good practices reduces effort. The challenge was not deleting processes, but to change them in a way that the intended results are achieved as quickly and cost-efficient as possible. If a process is applied by many employees, even small improvements can result in big savings.

All employees were invited to contribute to an improvement idea contest and special (money) awards were awarded to the best proposals.

Everyone was invited to contribute via the company intranet and a special mail that included a description of the topic which was sent to those responsible for the delivery process (project managers), bid management, presales, sales, competence management, as well as all process owners and the best innovators in the company.

Ideas were gathered on an internal tool, which contained a list of ideas and a short description of them. Ideas were closely monitored and a reminder mail was repeatedly sent containing already submitted ideas.

At the end, the results were good, far beyond targets. About half of invited persons from the target group sent proposals. The estimation for the implementation duration for proposals was: immediately for 12%; short-term for 42%; and long-term for 39% of proposals. For another 7% of proposals, additional analysis was still needed.

After the challenge, followed by announcements and news on the intranet portal, it was necessary to plan the implementation of unimplemented proposals, which was to be done in the next 12 months with monthly status monitoring.

Example: Simple improvement programme in an R&D business unit

There is a great example of a simple and straightforward improvement programme I saw in one business unit that generated many useful improvements over time.

A team was formed out of software developers working on a mature project with a bright future. There was a space for improvements in testing, log viewing and configuration reading. The improvement process was very simple: anyone with an idea should go straight to their superior and talk about the improvement. The idea was described later in a mail and improvement was tracked in developer's style – on the wiki.

This is the sentence explaining this process on the wiki:

> Projects here are where the "free-time" efforts of our team members go. A project here should bring either a direct business benefit (sell-able feature) or an indirect business benefit as a new utility (saving time) or should be stretching the skills of our team for new things.

Every idea on the wiki had only basic information: name, project owner, used Technologies, platform, status and repository. If the idea was realised it was also sent to the company's ideas programme to be recognised and awarded. A simple, but effective system.

16 Life After Agile

> Plans are useless, but planning is indispensable.   – Dwight D. Eisenhower

The development of agile, as the next step in the evolution of business methods after waterfall, is now widespread and well known. It is used all over the world in many adaptations, particularly among IT companies where it is a standard methodology.

What is the future? Will agile survive the rapid transformation of the business environment and workplace?

As already mentioned in the chapter "Life in the Agile World", agile was introduced for more effective, shortened processes; its first intention surely was not to promote innovation.

In innovative companies, the development teams should be allowed to assign time for developing innovations, which include ideas for new products, but also additions to the current portfolio, which will strengthen their market position. Failure tolerance is essential in any kind of innovation programme and it has the same importance if innovation is done in an agile environment. Also, innovative companies should encourage their employees to act like entrepreneurs. Most companies should adapt their current agile systems to all these needs now or in the near future.

What is the next step in the evolution of companies?

A great explanation of the current and future internal shapes of processes inside companies comes from the book *The Age of Surge*[64] by Brad Murphy and Dr. Carol Mase. They defined four waves of technological transformation. In the first wave (Collaboration), companies used agile methods and lean principles, which provided a doorway into technologies of wave 2 (Automation) where the use of cloud and automation infrastructure such as DevOps or Containers speeds up product development. In wave 3 (Orchestration) with the use of Micro Services or IoT, they see organisations using self-management and self-governing product management. Wave 4 (Augmented Intelligence), with the use of autonomous systems, self-organised products and services, and AI should lead to autonomous business units which are customer- and product-centric.

This approach can teach us a lot about future scenarios as waves 2 and 3 are currently operable, but wave 4 is still to come. But are companies in today's world decentralised and do ideas have a chance in today's agile oriented development process? Something clearly had to be changed to get ideas funded in the world where only customer-centric efforts are given funding.

---

[64] Brad Murphy, Dr. Carol Mase: The Age of Surge, A human Centered Framework for Scaling Company Wide Agility and Navigating the Tsunami of Digital, Reinvent Press, 2018.

https://doi.org/10.1515/9783110654448-016

In short, there is no big prediction. I can only say that agile and innovation together with all the technology changes upon us will form a new wave of business transformation and companies will again have to adapt and learn how to live in a new, changed world. This change is not coming in next 5 or 10 years – it is already here.

17 Every Engineer Needs a Businessman

I usually describe myself as an engineer; that's basically what I've been doing since I was a kid.
— Elon Musk

Do. Or do not. There is no try.
— Master Yoda[65]

The world as we know it may be run by businesspeople, but it is definitely shaped by engineers. Every engineer will say that the world will be a better place if tech guys made more decisions. In their own microcosm (organisation), they often rule, but how much help do they need from the non-tech side?

Inside corporations, engineers become managers (through experience and education provided in companies), which is natural – and as an engineer working in the software industry, where 90% of positions are held by engineers, I can say that things can surely work in that way – but what about in startups, where there's no time or budget for such an education?

Big ideas work best when there is a collaboration of disciplines; every Jobs needs a Wozniak, just as every Tesla needs a Westinghouse. And Tesla is a great example, he was the biggest inventor of the 20th century, and although he lived in a sea of corporate sharks, he had no interest in making a profit. Competitors copied or even stole some of his ideas. Without a "sponsor" he couldn't have commercialised his ideas and today we wouldn't be benefitting from them. Even the biggest minds need help.

Inside corporations, many innovators are introverts or simply don't have the courage or strength to fight for their ideas. Fear, inexperience, or just a lacking innovation culture inside the department or the whole organisation can block employees. So, corporate innovators need a sponsor – often their superior – on their side.

I'm often invited to give lectures at the economics department Entrepreneurship, and it is there that I face many questions from future entrepreneurs who are afraid of what the future holds for them. There is always the question of how to be successful and how to develop ideas. They think they can shape the concept, but have no tech knowledge to make it happen. So what can they do? The answer lies in collaboration. Simply put, businesspersons should have partners from the engineering profession and vice versa.

Many startups are growing in numbers, hiring software developers, but rarely business smarts. Later, the leader tries to learn skills that could come from a partner who studied management or entrepreneurship. This education can generate a great leader or innovator, but it can also be a fatal mistake for the future of the company. Many entrepreneurs are unable to push their ideas forward and have to put their dreams on hold, as they can't find a partner with the other needed skills.

---

65 In the film "The Empire Strikes Back", 1980.

https://doi.org/10.1515/9783110654448-017

The best solution is to educate technicians from the beginning with other non-tech skills and equip them with a bit of a business foundation. On the other hand, inside organisations and innovation programmes, technicians can be educated too. This could be done by holding a series of internal or external workshops with topics like business model generation, business planning, quick prototyping, writing a proof of concept, making an elevator pitch and so on. The education process can be done using internal power, but it can also be formatted using external help from universities, business schools or consultants. And that is where the main focus should be: every person in a software development environment should have a chance to become an internal entrepreneur. The right tools and skills should be available and part of the innovation or intrapreneurship process.

In the end, we should have a portion of employees who are businesspersons too and know not only how to shape, prototype and develop an idea, but also how to make a business plan or pitch.

Struggling startup

Recently, I saw an interesting example. A company was started with the intention of building a software project for a specific niche. The idea was excellent and two founders described the use case, business model and project plan for an idea. They both have knowledge in economics and finance and this was easy. They even presented the idea at a venture capital event and got great reviews. Initial capital was secured and they started to search for developers who would create their software platform.

First, they found a company that could develop the application, but this company couldn't secure enough resources. The next company was too expensive, and later, when they finally found developers they did the project without planning or following the development process. At the end, they left the project. Later, another group of developers continued with the project, but it was difficult to catch up, as they were already late.

At the time that I'm writing this, the company still has a good perspective, however, only the website is functioning. The founders are still waiting for the application to be finished.

This is an example where economists need a good technician to lead the software project, sort the milestones and break down the product timeline into phases and lead developers working on the project. Great ideas, brilliant founders and a niche that is waiting for this project may still not be enough to succeed.

Using non-technical skills

Everyone has several skills apart from the ones needed for a common everyday job – developers and other IT experts, too. Even as these skills are not needed in their everyday tasks, they should discover how to connect their non-technical skills with technical expertise, as these skills could be needed for innovation. The right place to do that is with education intended for the intrapreneurship process.

As technology disturbances create new jobs and also make some old tasks obsolete, it is necessary to sail into new waters. This means that one person can change many tasks, assignments or even jobs in a short time. Only persons with wider knowledge and interests will survive.

Traps for startups

According a recent study [66] the three main reasons why startups fail are:
- no market need
- run out of cash
- not the right team

No market need means that the problem that new product is solving is simply not stated in the right manner. A startup is solving one problem without understanding the bigger one that the customer really wants solved. Let's say that they are making a solution for shipments inside a logistics company and have made an application that will make it visible, but the real problem this company wants to solve is how to avoid late shipments.

Startups must be connected with the market from the start. Often, new companies are started when an expert finds a way to solve a problem in her field and steps out of the former company to make a new one in order to be able to provide this solution. This situation can be avoided by having an intrapreneurship programme inside the company, but let's now focus on a new startup. If the problem is well defined, this is a big step toward success.

All startups have limited fuel, as they run on resources which must somehow be provided to finish their product. They could get investments or simply be funded with founders' money, but someone (investor or founder) must be convinced of the idea. When founders are looking for investors, they must have the ability to present their product in the right way and, if possible, make initial prototypes to motivate investors. Of course (as described earlier), tech-experts would need managerial skills or they

---

66 cbs insights: The top 20 reasons why startups fail. https://www.cbinsights.com/research/startup-failure-reasons-top/.

must add someone with that profile to the team. The next thing is focus which is essential when there is a lack of resources, as time will surely run out fast (as always, but especially in the startup world), so only the right focus can lead to success.

Money allocation is something every startup founder has on their mind, but does everyone have the right skills for it? When a company is started, there is often no time for additional education. Then it is easier to add a person or reach for help from externals.

Could a startup do the whole project? Is the team right? Do they have market insights, which will guide the product to the right niche?

Many tasks are on the shoulders of founders like market validation, marketing, listening to customers, business modelling or pricing planning. All this should be done and everything is going so fast ... The key is (as always) having the right people. Also, good communication and harmony inside this small team must be achieved. If the team doesn't have it at the start, what will happen when it grows? Planning the project and sticking to reasonable milestones should avoid the risk of burnout, which could kill the project.

Finally, I must say that a startup idea has the same path, often with a much more difficult process than ideas born inside the companies. On the other hand, internal startups have a much easier path to success when looking for resources, but pretty much the same when looking at convincing investors (executives). It is a challenge to reach the market, get market insights or make prototypes, plan the resources needed and find the right people for these tasks. This could be much easier inside a company, but there can still be blocks, as company structures must allow internal entrepreneurship in an innovation-friendly atmosphere.

Next is an example of a successful internal startup.

Effipoint

Recently, I was involved in a startup challenge. We didn't have too much time, but the task was clear, the team was formed and we won! How?

A big multinational company whose business operations include the production, development, sales and distribution of consumer goods, with a simultaneous market presence in over 40 countries around the world, organised a regional startup challenge. The target was to make a solution for a logistics business and the scope was something like this:

> We want to digitally transform our delivery processes. Do you have an innovative solution that will provide added value added for our customers?

The company's distribution subsidiaries competed in difficult markets with relatively low margins. Any increase in supply chain efficiency significantly affected the bottom line. Further on, innovations in customer service allow them to remain the market leader and differentiate among other distributors of a similar profile.

In other words, their business case was a digital transformation of their delivery processes.

We formed a team, a kind of internal startup, composed of two mentors and two students and after being introduced to the targets and software platform, which was part of the challenge, we started to think about a solution.

A month later we won, even though the competition included different software firms from several European countries, which – believe it or not – already had products on the market. The decision board said that our application offered unique innovative features and that "we had run an extra mile" in this competition.

We did it by building a software prototype (an application) that included all major functionalities and features and then we created a 3-minute video with a presentation showing all aspects of our solution. Everything was done in a fast, self-organising way, constantly learning new technologies (software tools) and exploring a new business area of transportation.

Our strength was in a different approach; we tried to think differently (lateral) and to offer something that was not yet known or offered in this field. Also, we looked at the problem from the customer's side and did some investigating into the challenges from the customer's perspective, which was crucial to understanding the problem – let's say that was just a bit of design thinking. Introducing artificial intelligence, having transparency in the communication channels, using big data processing power and machine learning were highlighted and we simply won the challenge.

The team was mixed and included a senior solution architect, innovation specialist and students from a local college. We believe that this created the flow of new ideas from different angles. In the end, we were satisfied with our prototype and so were the customer and challenge-starter.

Of course, the main challenges were still ahead. Later, the product evolved and was offered on the market. The product was reshaped and it has a nice future, as logistics and AI make a nice pair.

18 Startups

I skate to where the puck is going to be, not where it has been.   – Wayne Gretzky

Startups are started around a business idea. They are led by the vision of the founders (as an example of a top-down approach) and often, if successful, they start with
rapid growth. During that growth period, they need to reinvent themselves and
start making some internal processes. An important process should be how to handle innovations in an environment that is no longer five but 155 people.

Fast-growing startups face the challenge that when their product reaches the
peak of growth and when it's needed to input a new life or add the new product to
the company's portfolio (as shown in Figure 18.1). Redefinition of the product or of
the whole company should be started as soon as possible to avoid the state of de-
pression. An example for that process is the use of a lean startup and pivoting.

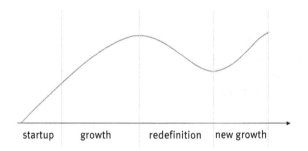

Figure 18.1: Startup lifecycle.

It must be said that startups have the advantage over older companies as they are
building their hardware and software capabilities from zero, while companies always have some "historical reasons" which could cause delays or not supported elements that would tear down chances of new products.

Let's take a look at examples of startups.

Rovio

Case 1: Summer 2013, at 6 p.m. I'm home after work and relaxing with my then
6- and 4-year-old sons. We're lying on the balcony and everyone is playing the
same game on their iPhones or iPad: Angry Birds.

Case 2: Sunday morning and one of the boys just realised what day it is today –
it's the day the new Angry Birds Toon is available! Let's see the new episode!

https://doi.org/10.1515/9783110654448-018

You already figured out that I'm a fan, but let's dive deeper into the Angry Birds makers' philosophy. The Finnish firm Rovio is the creator of this mega-popular brand started several years ago with a smartphone game.

When the game was launched, developers spread the word about the game to friends with iPhones (in Nokia-based Finland there weren't too many iPhones in those days). The game quickly become number one in the Finnish AppStore. During the Winter Olympics, one Swedish skier had an accident and during the TV interview, he said that it will be very boring to sit alone in the hotel room, but fortunately, he has Angry Birds on his phone! After the interview the game reached number one in the Swedish AppStore. The next stops were the UK and USA... When the game reached number one in the AppStore, it stayed there for 300 days.

So how did Rovio make it? Before Angry Birds they had 51 games, so they learned a lot from previous projects and analysed hundreds of games before this big launch. Also, the ecosystem was too hostile for a startup before the AppStore launch. Simply put, the market wasn't ready before AppStore. It's important to mention that the text was eliminated from the game and they made it easy to understand the game and play it. Much time was given to details – there were 30 different designs alone for an App Icon.

The fastest-growing brand is not only the game; now it's the large range of physical products and also cartoons. Rovio created the biggest animation studio in Northern Europe – they launched one cartoon a week. Overnight, they reached an audience of 1.7 billion people who have at least one of the Angry Birds games on their device. Astonishing, isn't it?

I was happy to be in their headquarters in Espoo, Finland, and had the opportunity to ask some questions. What I thought to ask was reflecting on "Case 1" from the beginning of this article: Why can't Angry Birds be played against other players? But then I remembered that few weeks in the past, Angry Birds Friends was on the market! Well, Rovio was ahead of their fans, and surely ahead of me!

The next thing for Rovio was educational books, activity parks, Angry Birds films. Rovio is alive, Angry Birds are still on my iPhone, and new films are on track ...

Photomath

Any parent anywhere in the world who wants to quickly check math homework, or any student who needs to check the procedure for their math assignment, surely knows about Photomath. Photomath[67] is an educational tool for a smartphone or tablet, and with over 100 million downloads, is one of the most popular educational

---

67 https://www.photomath.net/en/.

apps of all times. It solves math problems and helps with homework assignments for millions of students and pupils across the world.

The success of this app is tied to its founder Damir Sabol, a serial entrepreneur who started with an internet provider company and now is focused on Microblink, the company that deals with the research and development of software products in the field of computer vision on mobile phones. Photomath is from 2016. It separated from Microblink. He defines himself more as an initiator then investor who wants to experiment and start actions based on new technologies.[68] It is necessary that the startup solve a problem, preferably 10 times better than the problem was solved earlier, and if you are first with the solution, you can have a very successful startup. A functional prototype, product-market fit and traction gets performance potential, which increases chances for funding. As the costs of technological development are very high, it is possible (but rare) that startups try to make products that are globally relevant and which customers are willing to pay a good amount for and that this income will finance further development. Additionally, profitable growth must be supported inside the company, which must provide a quality product and good service.

His company made PhotoPay, an application that scans bills, recognises text, amount and offers one-click payment.

The idea for Photomath was born one evening when Damir corrected his son's math homework.[69] There were a lot of tasks, and he was tired. Too tired to calculate. "If our application can read payouts, why would not it be able to read and solve math tasks?" he thought. The next day he was at work talking to a team of engineers about his idea. The first response was that it was difficult to make and had no gigantic potential. They didn't work on ideas until 2014. Microsoft had opened the contests for Windows Phone apps. Developers just needed to present ideas and they would get resources for development. They applied, got resources and started working on the app.

The concept was very simple. A cell phone user scans a printed job, and the application offers a solution to the procedure. An early version did not work that well and it wasn't finished, but somehow it did work (more like a technology showcase). It was available exclusively for Windows phones for three months, with no big interest (only a few hundred downloads). Damir, however, signed up for TechCrunch Disrupt with Photomath. Now, the app would be available for other operating systems. Damir decided that it would be free, as at the time he did not think he had a product that was worth the billing. The application was defective and he saw it only as a technological demonstration. His main product was the technology for paying the bills (PhotoPay). Photomath was supposed to be a marketing tool for PhotoPay. They knew that when the application would be available on other operating systems,

68 https://privredni.hr/damir-sabol.
69 https://www.telegram.hr/price/s-26-je-iz-podruma-napravio-iskon-onda-se-slomio-i-povukao-a-danas-ima-aplikaciju-koju-je-skinulo-40-milijuna-ljudi/.

and when it would be shown on TechCrunch, the number of downloads would jump. They thought that the ultimate reach of Photomath would be 50,000–100,000 downloads.

On the first day of the conference, Photomath entered the top four applications. They were in the media, and on the first day it was available on all operating systems, the application was downloaded by 50,000 people. On the second day, they were on half a million downloads. On the third day a million. After a month, 5 million people had downloaded the app. Today, there are more than 150 million downloads, and every day more then 35 millions of math problems are solved.

The biggest win in this project was to create a unique programming language that serves the technology behind the application to make this process possible. All procedures for solving these problems are then written in that language. Machine learning is used for reading signs from the picture and an AI expert system is used for solving tasks.[70]

Their future mission is to provide mathematical knowledge to anyone anywhere in the world whenever they need it. By combining its own technology for text recognition (OCR) and its own Math Engine to solve math problems, Photomath simulates the process of solving how teachers do it. The tasks are broken down into simple and straightforward steps that allow the user to understand basic mathematical concepts. In this way, the user is able to independently identify the course material, check the assignment, or acquire new knowledge. Some of the new features are geometry-solving and word-written tasks, and users can also choose from several methods of solving specific tasks that have this option.

In fact, building and enhancing the capabilities of the app has been going on for five years, with more than 120 people currently working at the company, most of whom are engaged in content development and creation. In its offices in Zagreb and California, Photomath brings together machine learning experts, software engineers, math teachers, UI and UX designers, QA experts, data engineers, marketers and many others.

This is an example where the vision of the founder and his ability to pivot made a startup globally recognised and successful. Also, this example shows that it is still possible to be first in the world with a unique idea.

Corporations and startups

Siemens has a separate unit to foster disruptive ideas more vigorously and to accelerate the development of new technologies. The unit's name, "next47," arises from the fact that Siemens was founded in 1847. At next47, the company is pooling its

---

70 PhotoMath Fact Sheet https://photomath.net/presskit/Photomath_fact_sheet.pdf.

existing startup activities. The unit is open to employees as well as to founders, external startups and established companies if they want to pursue business ideas in the company's strategic innovation fields.[71] At next47, they put the entrepreneur at the centre; by unlocking the Siemens ecosystem and tapping into its global network of customers, they help grow its customer base and get new customers faster. In short, they are trying to bridge the gap between innovation and implementation.[72]

---

[71] next47: Siemens founds separate unit for startups. https://press.siemens.com/global/en/fea ture/next47-siemens-founds-separate-unit-startups.
[72] next47 A new approach to innovation https://next47.com/approach.

19 Be Original

If you're not prepared to be wrong, you'll never come up with anything original.

– Sir Ken Robinson

It's always important to be the pioneer in some field, no matter what industry we are talking about. Software companies and startups must be really fast or as another option, find a new way to deal with the old problem – to be original in a world where everyone wants to have a unique idea.

But how to achieve that?

Startups will simply die if their idea has many drawbacks or if it's not recognised by customers. Things could be over pretty quickly. On the other hand, established companies which are trying to get new ideas on the market must be careful when investing and be ready to fail. The way established companies could find new originality is through education of its employees, as expanding knowledge means expanding the chances for new insights. The help can also come by setting up a kind of technology management activities. Some of them, market and trends scanning, together with thinking of future scenarios, will surely ignite new thoughts and educating people will make these thoughts become reality. Not the easiest task, but it's achievable.

For the individual, originality comes from questioning everything around them. Why is this process done in that way? Why is this product feature done that way? Why are different customers asking for the same thing, even though we think they don't need it?

The next starter of originality is to have many ideas. True innovators, of course, know it, but do all software engineers in the company know how to handle many ideas, how to store them and later come back to them?

Being original can only be achieved by having deep expertise in some field, knowledge of how to realise the idea and some luck at the end. Many startup stories provide such an example. Facebook wasn't the first idea for such kind of social network, but it had its own originality and a unique story from the start.

Here are two examples of how original ideas and hard work made a successful product, which ultimately created a successful company.

Nordeus and Top Eleven

Nordeus was started in a flat.[73]After a few days, three founders rented a space which had no windows and they stayed there for half a year. Started in 2009,

---

73 https://startit.rs/branko-i-milan-iz-nordeusa-igramo-da-pobedimo/.

https://doi.org/10.1515/9783110654448-019

working 14–16 hours and 7 days a week with no breaks, they took their first holiday only for Christmas 2010.

They didn't want to waste any time as they had an idea for a very popular segment in gaming and there wasn't anything similar on Facebook at that time. Their product was Top Eleven – an online football manager game developed for Facebook and mobile devices – the game is still available and still has millions of active players.

From the start, they had the task of building all processes by adapting them to their needs with procedures working for a small startup, but also adaptable for scaling to 20, 50 or 100 people. With company culture relying on teamwork and a winning mentality, they succeeded in their task. Now, they have several games in their portfolio and a new headquarters as the company has grown and is now well placed in the gaming industry.

Infobip

Silvio Kutić finished a degree in electrical engineering and computing and immediately got a job in the state's electro-energetics company. He came to work one Monday morning, worked for 4 hours, went on break, drank some coffee and bought a bus ticket to his hometown. He quit a secure job and never returned. Instead, he started a different path in his hometown Vodnjan, where he created a local business-oriented social network with a group of friends, all talented developers in the year 2002.[74]

This startup project aimed at transforming the Vodnjan local community into a digital municipality, and allowed them to recognise the potential of SMS.[75] They wanted to connect people and local businesses, allowing them to communicate with one another over a web app, email, and SMS messaging. The project failed, but they learned from it and launched the web application Infobip. Silvio and his colleague, Izabel Jelenić, registered a company with the same name.

The company made its first business deal for delivering 14,000 SMS greeting cards to the entire city. It worked, and they recognised the business potential of A2P (application-to-person) SMS and they focused on it. The system was focused on text messages sent from CRM systems, banking applications, reservation systems and other business applications, to persons. If you receive SMS from your bank, insurance company, retail chain, taxi service, or a reply to you after you voted for your favourite on a television show – chances are that this message landed on your cell phone via Infobip. They added channels like Facebook Messenger, Viber and email. They entered the fields of artificial intelligence, chatbots and the Internet of Things (IoT). The

---

74 Infobip, About Us https://www.infobip.com/en/about.
75 Silvana Međušić, Telegram: https://www.telegram.hr/price/nakon-faksa-se-zaposlio-u-elektri-prvi-dan-dao-otkaz-sad-u-vodnjanu-ima-globalnu-firmu-s-1200-ljudi/.

customer base is measured in the billions, and through Infobip's platform, more than 60% of the world's mobile phones, or four billion people, were contacted by 2018. Each month, more than six billion messages are delivered through their platform. They built a platform, not product-by-product, but learning from others, too. Their formula for success is that they found a good niche and good associates, constantly corrected, listened to customer and market needs, and pivoted.

Today, they have a new headquarters with 17,000 square meters in a town with a population of just 3,000 people, more than 60 offices worldwide and more than 600 successful operator partnerships.

Infobip's values:

> We are the HUMBLE ENGINEERS led by our philosophy of LEARNING BY DOING and fueled by our PASSION FOR TECHNOLOGY. We value CREATIVITY, PERSISTENCE and INNOVATION.
>
> INTEGRITY and living MEANINGFUL LIVES are the FOUNDATIONS of ALL OUR VALUES.

Many things can be learned from this example. We can see here a strong determination to succeed, high-quality trend spotting for this sector and then meeting the challenge to lead a niche and widening the portfolio inside it. This is also an example of one idea that made a startup, which led to a big company that is spread all over the world. What is more important, it was done from a really small town in a remote part of a small European country.

Copycats

There are many companies whose whole business strategy is to find a successful product in a foreign market, be the first in copying it, and then place it on a domestic or regional market. This could work and there are sometimes even examples of copycats making a more successful product than the original, as they built on it and made a long-lasting business. But these companies also need the strengths of a well-placed entity to place, promote and create such products. Such companies need special technology management skills – to recognise and transform ideas from other environments.

But one question remains open, the question of the stolen idea: What if someone steals your idea?

Stolen idea

What happens if your idea is stolen?

You have an idea. Your great, wonderful idea, which is the best thing anyone has heard in years or centuries ... Your pet project, your way to say goodbye to company life and start your own startup. On the other hand, it can be your project inside the company, which will make you the recognised intrapreneur. As many other innovators, you explain your idea to your friends, colleagues or superiors trying to get funding or valuable feedback. But then, weeks or months later, you found out that someone realised your idea without your permission.

There are so many similar stories and the point is that often you can't do much except to feel miserable and helpless.

But (on the other hand), why steal in the first place?

First, we need to know that we are not all innovators and that some people are just better in finding new ideas or projects, while others are struggling with their creativity and can only copy or steal (or do nothing). Some people don't have enough knowledge or imagination (or both) to be creative in a way that it would produce a successful idea, their only approach is to copy or even to steal. But, first what is the difference between stealing and copying? You can copy only an already finished product, published work or realised idea. On the other hand, ideas that are not yet known to the public, like products that are still in the works or not yet published. If these works are copied, they are just – stolen.

Next, is it really a good idea to take someone's idea?

A stolen idea is a closed box. An "idea thief" doesn't know that there may be some other related ideas behind it. What could be the next features? Which combinations can be done with other sectors of the market? Also, the innovator was in a certain state-of-mind when the idea was born and she can recall this memory (or at least try to recall it) and sometimes continue in the same direction as during the time of idea generation. Simply put, the ideator can remember the time when she was in "the zone" and by reflecting on those memories can draw new ideas for further shaping of the original idea. On the other hand, the "idea thief" can't have this possibility. Also, the innovator knows how this idea could grow and how the next project could be built upon this idea, maybe even how the idea can be connected with other already known or still to be developed products or ideas.

A "thief" or copycat will never find these things out and a stolen idea often remains in the shape it had at the beginning without any new valuable additions. In short, an idea thief can never know all the future possibilities and scenarios of the original idea that the innovator already has in his head (or in her notebook).

> I don't care that they stole my idea … I care that they don't have any of their own. – Nikola Tesla

So, if your idea is stolen, you still have a chance to make a better project or product than the "thief". Just, don't hesitate to start over, make it unique – or different than the copycat and beat her in the market.

If this happens inside a company, the first person to contact is an innovation manager who must have control and insights into every idea which exists or existed inside the company. Every idea inside some environment has its author, name and date of submission – this should be enough to determine its first creator and solve the problem.

20 Mechanisms for Success

> The only way to do great work is to love what you do.   – Steve Jobs

To give innovation additional chances other than top-down or bottom-up initiatives, and to find new business models, further mechanisms could be established (as shown in Figure 20.1). A company could offer its innovators the chance to realise their ideas through a corporate incubator. It could acquire new businesses, cooperate with other companies through joint ventures, allow spin-offs for internal startups so they can live on their own, or reach to the world via open innovation. Let's take a closer look at these approaches.

Corporate incubators

One way to isolate, nurture and support innovators is through corporate incubators. In a software company, it is not easy to achieve this and get these kinds of resources – to take engineers away from their everyday work and place them on innovation projects, which will last mid- or long-term. Incubators should be physically separated from other parts of the company and innovators must feel the support and faith that executives are giving them in their endeavour to get new ideas to the market. Appropriate personalities with a range of different skills should provide a healthy and prosperous atmosphere guided by the person responsible for innovation. These product teams should then manage their activities by themselves, but supervised by the innovation manager.

Corporate innovation centres are examples of how to nurture innovation in corporations. An example is the SAP Innovation Center Network,[76] where multidisciplinary teams from six locations worldwide are exploring emerging technologies to define their value and to solve industry problems.

Spin-offs

If the new project grows and has a future, but it grows beyond the borders set by the parent corporation, we may have a candidate for a spin-off. The decision to let go of a project is made if it is not suitable for the market currently supported by the company, or simply if the executives do not support the project, but the project leader thinks it can have a further life outside the organisation. In that case, the

---

76 https://icn.sap.com.

https://doi.org/10.1515/9783110654448-020

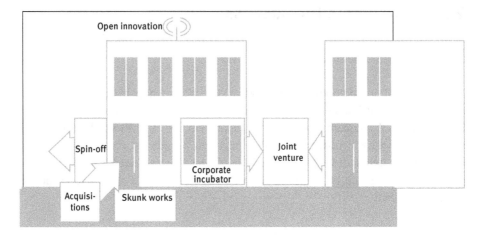

Figure 20.1: Innovation mechanisms.

project must be prepared for its next life by ensuring that no boundaries are set by the mother corporation. The new startup must be prepared for its new life.

There are many software companies that have ceased to exist today, and we can learn a lot from their disappearance. What happened to Altavista, Netscape or Napster? On the other hand, why have some companies become so successful? What is the story behind Netflix or Instagram? How did Facebook or Google become so huge and still remain on track after a decade or two?

The first point is competition, as many companies are simply run over by the competition if they fail to adapt quickly and take steps which can save them.

An interesting story is Pixar's film "The Good Dinosaur". After three years in development, and only a few months before its scheduled release, they lost confidence in it. The decision was to push the release date back by 18 months and redo the film from scratch.[77] It was a big decision with an important statement and the success that followed.

Skunk works

Skunk Works refers to innovation activities that are done undercover (hidden from management) until their realisation. Teams or business units have time to create a new tool or feature for a known product, but there is no way to proceed with global plans. It is done with no big words, but after its realisation, it is promoted to higher

---

77 Oliver Franklin-Wallis: How Pixar embraces a crisis, Wired UK http://www.wired.co.uk/maga zine/archive/2015/12/features/pixar-embraces-crisis-the-good-dinosaur.

instances. It is done in cases where there is no chance of getting support from above, or there is simply no time to allocate the needed resources through the known system – this is something that should not happen in innovation-minded organisations. There is always a need for a sponsor – a person who will support skunk works – a team leader for small improvements or a department leader for ideas with a wider scope. This sponsor must act as a protector and the biggest supporter until the project is revealed.

Acquisitions

Bigger companies are buying startups or smaller companies (or the reverse – smaller, successful companies are buying larger ones) to gain access to the latest technology and knowledge possessed by their staff. It is a quick and safe way to get new knowledge and widen a company's portfolio. The new venture may be integrated into an existing business unit, but it may also be semi-independent as a new department inside the new organisation. This new venture should bring new life (if it is needed) to corporate culture and some of its good spirits. Even the innovation climate could overflow to other parts of the company.

Joint ventures

Joint ventures happen when two or more companies join together to make a new entity where they will cooperate and derive new value from it. This is also a chance to experiment, make new products or just have a place where externals could help with new inventions or ideas which should be part of future endeavours.

Open innovation

Open innovation is a topic on its own and it will need much space to be elaborated. I will give only give a quick overview here and extend it with an example.

Looking outside of companies' borders for ideas is a challenging way to widen their perspective and allow externals to introduce their thoughts inside company. Open innovation as a strategy is used to connect those external sources with internal experts and place those efforts within an established innovation process. This approach can be a great help in absorbing external ideas and expertise. It is also used for providing knowledge from an area where the company's experts don't have experience or just have weak points. This principle could add additional brain power to the necessary tasks or topics.

There are many examples of open innovation challenges that have run in recent times. The Nokia Open Innovation Challenge[78] asked companies to propose products and solutions within one domain to an international jury. The Kaspersky Open Innovation Programme[79] invited innovative startups to support the growth of new joint business activities.

Next are the examples of two open innovation challenges held by big IT companies; there are many similarities, but also some unique aspects to both approaches.

NTT DATA Open Innovation Contest

NTT DATA is a global IT innovator with business operations in more than 50 countries and regions. They provide professional services from consulting and system development to business IT outsourcing.[80]

They holds an annual international Open Innovation Contest (in 2019 they started the 10th edition) where they invite startup businesses around the globe to submit ideas for new technologies that can make the world a better place. Regional contests are held in 15 cities across 13 countries worldwide, with 1–2 winner(s) in different business challenges being chosen. The motto of the contest is "Let's change the world together".[81] They are looking for startups that are ready to scale up and are mature enough to partner with a big corporation to co-create innovation. Startups can offer solutions to specific challenges in eight domains: healthcare and life sciences, finance, insurance and payments, automotive, telecom and IoT, in-storefront and marketing digitalisation, smart automation, data distribution and disruptive social innovation.

The process starts by submitting an application and documentation. This is followed by a screening phase and a pitch day in every city (final regional screening by pitching at each location). The next phase is acceleration where contest hosts work with the winners to maximise the business opportunity. After six months, the grand finale takes place where all regional winners gather in Tokyo to give their final pitches and then the grand champion is selected.

Red Hat Open Innovation Labs

Red Hat, a multinational software company providing open-source software products to the enterprise community, uses Open Innovation Labs to catalyse innovation:

78 Nokia Open Innovation Challenge 2019 https://www.nokia.com/innovation/open-innovation-challenge-2019/.
79 Kaspersky Open Innovations Program https://www.kaspersky.com/blog/open-innovation/.
80 NTT DATA Company profile https://www.nttdata.com/global/en/about-us/company-profile.
81 NTT DATA Open Innovation Contest 10 http://oi.nttdata.com/en/contest/.

Learn to build software the Red Hat way, during an immersive residency, in a space designed for speed and innovation.[82]

The thought that teams in IT are innovating faster and improving quality with DevOps is propagated here. So, they created a space for innovation to happen – Innovation Labs:
- Try. Learn. Modify.
- Fail fast – or win quickly.
- It is okay to not know everything in advance.

They use open source tools and culture in order to make innovation happen. First, the team of externals works with Red Hat mentors for 1–3 months and makes a prototype using the necessary infrastructure and software tools in a space "where it's safe to test a hypothesis, learn from the results, and modify the approach". Their approach is to break big things into smaller parts; they avoid long-term planning, but instead automate, build new skills and experiment.

---

82 Red Hat Open Innovation Labs – Catalyze Innovation Ebook – https://www.redhat.com/en/services/consulting/open-innovation-labs.

21 7innovation Method

> There are different ways to do innovation. You can plant a lot of seeds, not be committed to any particular one of them, but just see what grows. And this really isn't how we've approached this. We go mission-first, then focus on the pieces we need and go deep on them and be committed to them.
> – Mark Zuckerberg

Let's summarise what we have seen so far concerning relationships between three basic types of ideas in regard to sensitivity to rewards, capability for innovation challenges, openness to everyone in the company, additional effort needed for building capacity, and relationship to innovation climate:

	Improvements	Innovations	Inventions
Sensibility to rewards	+	?	+
Capability for innovation challenges	+	+	?
Everyone /everywhere	+	?	−
Effort for building capacity	−	+	+
Related to innovation climate	−	+	−

Figure 21.1: Insights into basic types of ideas.

How do you make the innovation process simpler, more efficient and more successful?

I'll try to explain it here using the term "7innovation" as the method uses seven steps in introducing innovation principles. It is a method that encapsulates the innovation challenge "call for ideas" explained in the chapter "Innovation Challenges" and it also uses insights from Figure 21.1. The method is the result of my experience with the innovation process and what I have seen in other IT companies.

The "7innovation method" focuses on making the innovation process fast and responsive to short-term goals. What makes this method unique is the recognition of the iterative access with a deep scan of an organisation's capabilities (including internal innovators) as the greatest source of creativity in any organisation.

This method may be briefly explained as starting by setting up an innovation culture and then holding innovation contests and/or innovation workshops. This may be called the **awakening** phase (shown in Figure 21.2). After that, much data is collected

https://doi.org/10.1515/9783110654448-021

and the best innovators (let's say "thinkers") are selected (**Selection**). The contest is then done narrowly and well defined (**Contest**). **Scanning** ideas and using selection criterion during a project's initial phase is a normal part of any innovation process **(Decision)**. After **realisation**, it is essential to include a **storytelling** phase to positively market the success story.

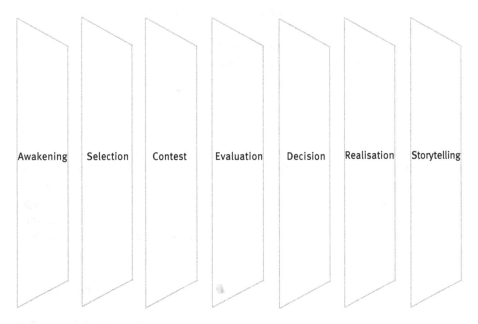

Awakening Selection Contest Evaluation Decision Realisation Storytelling

Figure 21.2: The 7innovation method.

Now, let's dig deep inside this method. The starting point, or "**awakening**" phase of the process, is to launch an initial contest after getting C-level support, with the purpose of "feeling the pulse" of the organisation and discovering innovative persons.

This contest may have a broad topic related to future strategy, which could appeal to future innovators to unleash their creativity. An example is starting the challenge with wide topic like possible future strategy of the company (that could become a new portfolio element). The competition would be open to everyone inside the organisation, and the topic description should be simple and always visible.

At this point, the main goal is to encourage a number of ideas, but later on, there will be several decision gates, which will filter the best ideas for implementation. As in any innovation process, a successful idea must also generate a success story, which will be the generator for further innovation activities. After holding such a contest, the data collected will help in the next phase of "**Selection**". This phase can be skipped if similar activities have already been done and there is data about the best internal innovators. This initial phase should be used to learn about the strong and weak parts of the process, and about the problems innovators or intrapreneurs have getting their idea prototyped or even implemented.

To make the "7innovation method" sustainable, it is most important to keep innovators informed and to be able to select the best ideators as part of the "innovation team". It is important to keep in mind that the best innovators are not the ones who submit the most ideas, but the ones who can "think differently" and present ideas whose quality can be "felt".

To set up an innovation **"Contest"**, we'll first need a topic that is clearly defined, and aligned with company strategy with a focus on market demands. Ideally, this should be a "trendy" topic or problem that has the ability to push innovators to engage in the contest. The sales, marketing, management or customer teams can generate a new topic in areas that need new ideas from the "innovation team" we have set up. Product owners, as the link between development and business, may also have their thoughts when determining the topic. The topic needs to be well described with thoughts on the current customer situation. Technical details should be sparse, as this could lead innovators down the wrong path. It must be said that ideas don't need details in this phase – general concepts are better and enough. Later the concept will be shaped and polished and it will offer much more information than the initial idea. It doesn't need to be detailed, but it does need to be flexible, as there is a long road ahead; it should, however, have an answer to the initial problem and a way to reach a solution.

If rewards are offered, the amounts and rules must be clearly stated side-by-side near the initiative's topic explanation.

The "contest leader" must provide quick support to innovators in case of any questions. Transparency is very important – a simple way to do this is to create a place (intranet or website) where all submitted ideas are visible so that innovators can be inspired by the ideas of others. Ideas must be explained briefly and be understandable.

In this phase, quantity is also needed, so the more ideas we have, the better. Every innovator should know that. The right topic with an excellent description and the right people on the "innovation team" should generate a quantity of ideas of good quality. Once innovators are interested by looking at the ideas of others and submitting their own ideas, they should be kept engaged by promoting the best ideas using reminder mails, news about the innovation tool or similar methods.

When the innovation contest is finished, with the ideas written and listed on a table on the company's intranet or some idea generation tool, a new chapter is opened called **"Evaluation"**. So, how do you decide which ideas should be eliminated and which should be elaborated upon? At this point, it is vital to involve the right people, such as decision-makers. These could be market specialists or innovation/trend spotters as evaluators, along with people who have a budget – product managers or executives. The criteria could be just "like it"/"don't like it" or (better) a detailed approach valuing criteria like "close to trends", "alignment with portfolio", "market need", "feasibility" or "applicable in short term". How much will it cost to realise the idea and how much value will the idea bring in the end? Of course, the current portfolio must be scanned in such a way as to see which of the submitted proposals could fit, or be a part of existing portfolio elements. There must be a place in the company's portfolio of products for innovation. Ideas must fit with skills and knowledge already available, or that can be set in the next period of time. It must be said that every idea should have the same chance, and all ideas have to be presented in the same way. The scores of all evaluators should be added up and presented. Additionally, it could be extended with an integrated social media voting system where everyone could vote and a summary of the votes could be then added to the votes of the decision-makers.

The organisation has to know its capabilities and strategy in order to determine the fate of ideas. Of course, only ideas that can be implemented internally should be accepted. After screening and evaluation, a **"Decision"** has to be made about which ideas will move forward. The innovator has to be at the centre of this phase, even though other colleagues may join in this new project. This could be the point where the innovation team is formed (it could also be done earlier if needed, or if there was a team of innovators behind the ideas from the start).

After establishing a budget, the idea officially becomes a project and is treated as any other similar work in an organisation, which leads to **"Realisation"**. The project gets funding for the first phase (it should be planned in phases), and after a successful initial phase, the next budget is realised. It is important to have funding done in stages to minimise risk. As the project matures with time, new learning and offerings should bring the project to safety, allowing for the allocation of a larger budget.

If successful, the last phase should be sharing the success of this story. **"Storytelling"** is very important for sustaining an innovation culture and for the internal marketing of an idea system in an organisation. There is no better inspiration for joining in innovation initiatives than the success of a co-worker who experienced that her idea was realised in that very same environment.

The process must reinvent itself according to the reshaping or growing of the company. Things should be constantly improved and every new challenge must be unique. If the process is exciting and participants feel the joy of innovating, then the first goal has been reached.

Innovation community

With insights into innovation challenges, no innovation manager finds it a difficult task to recognise the best innovators in the company. They should make a community of an appropriate size for future tasks. Innovators inside the community can be reached anytime with new innovation challenges or even given the task of evaluating some proposals. They should be motivated and skilled to help innovation managers inside the company at anytime.

Linking innovators can lead to new ideas and proposals; when their expertise and creativity collide, surely many new ideas will be born. The established environment (ecosystem) will allow collaboration and sharing of ideas that should bring new value to the organisation. A budget for time and stimulation must be available, but as this will not even be started without the support from the top, the problem should not be the lack of a budget, but the allocation of it to the right projects. Rewarding top innovators in specially broadcasted events and spreading the news through the organisation is a chance to attract new candidates to the innovation community, which should be growing over time.

The innovation community should be exclusive inside the company, but sometimes all other employees can join innovation activities like innovation challenges. Together this should make a company a proud innovator, but also a great place to work.

Metrics

Results will not come immediately. Only after two or three challenges will it be possible to measure the impact this process has on the organisation. To have strong results from innovation projects (future products), it is necessary to wait even longer.

Even more difficult to measure are the value, knowledge and skills[83] created by the education of innovators on their way to becoming entrepreneurs, and the level of innovation culture in an organisation. Some aspects can just be felt, not measured, but will executives be satisfied with this answer?

Usually, the first financial metric for innovation is generated revenue or cost reduction (mostly for improvements), but is it the right metric?

Many non-financial metrics are applicable and could point to the important things in the innovation process such as stage development which measures how many ideas have gone through various stages of the process. The next are the number of ideas generated and the number of realised projects, which could point to the level of innovation culture, together with the ratio of employees included in innovation activities. Return on investment (ROI) or other financial

---

83 Susana Jurado Apruzzese: Intrapreneurship: 10 lessons from the trenches, Core Innovation – Telefonica Innovation, March 2019.

metrics can work in well-established and mature innovation systems, mostly in large companies.

Communication

All phases of the process must be supported by intranet or another internal communications platform. Stage news, statistics, team case stories or advice should be available in order to inspire further engagement. News must follow each stage of the innovation challenge, as it is essential to keep the process transparent. The challenge should have its own website with every available piece of information, including videos from team production or from final events. Videos should include idea generation practices as inspiration for future participants. The website should have a bunch of resources and techniques, and it should be a place for support, but also for inspiration. Tutorials and online training could be another part of the platform and could create a kind of training repository.

All ideas must be documented, as this will make it possible to come back to an idea, maybe in next challenge, or simply help everyone understand that each idea matters and that they will be kept in the system together with all respective data.

Iterate

Innovation challenges should be done two to three times per year (or more) to achieve a constant influx of ideas into the system. There may be a situation in which an innovation challenge results in zero innovation projects and then the system is blocked until new ideas come in. This can be avoided by doing regular iterations to ensure that new ideas are in the system and also to include ideas from previous challenges as they mature.

Example: Telefonica – intrapreneurship with stage-gate and lean startup

Telefónica, S.A. is a multinational telecommunications company headquartered in Madrid, Spain. It is one of the largest telephone operators and mobile network providers in the world. It provides fixed and mobile telephony, broadband and subscription television, operating in Europe and the Americas.

In 2012, after applying the lean startup methodology to a couple of innovation projects and to an ideation programme already in place, the company redefined their innovation model, turning this methodology into their core way of working by turning innovation projects into internal ventures. Simultaneously, they began launching innovation calls. This is how LeanElephants, an intrapreneurship programme at Telefónica, was born.[84]

Here is what the Lean Elephants programme looks like now:

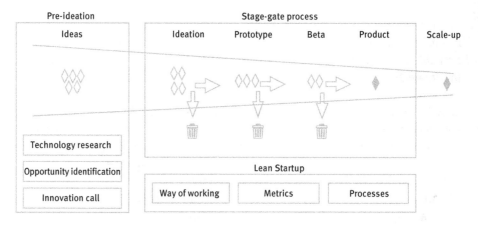

Figure 21.3: Lean Elephants programme.

This the result of several evolutions, after learning by testing different things and based on the needs that have been identified or have arisen at Telefónica. The pillars of the programme are:

- Lean startup is what defines the processes and the way of working in the company's ventures, as well as the metrics with which they measure their progress.
- They defined five different stages for their ventures and a stage-gating process to move from one stage to the next in a very similar way to the financing rounds of the venture capital world.
- To nurture an innovation funnel, they rely on innovation calls, where employees submit their ideas around the opportunity areas identified for company, and if they get selected, they are allowed to work full-time on their ideas.

They launched the 10Fridays initiative (ideation programme) where people submit ideas and get 10 Fridays to work on them.

The first effects of this programme were a 45% increase in the number of innovation projects and a 48% reduction in the average budget of innovation projects.

---

84 Susana Jurado Apruzzese: Intrapreneurship: 10 lessons from the trenches, Core Innovation – Telefonica Innovation.

22 Do Nothing in Dark Times?

If you always do what you always did, you will always get what you always got. –Albert Einstein

Every company has ups and downs in its lifecycle; this is particularly true with IT companies. In every lifecycle, after the start and then a period of expansion when the company is driven by its lead product(s), there comes a time of stability or stable growth, but after some time this naturally comes to an end. The era of the slowdown is then in effect. If companies haven't done innovation or portfolio change activities at the right time, this slowdown could last. For established companies, this is a cyclical process, which may occur every few years.

For innovation heroes in companies, this time of slowdown could be marked as a period of dark times. What to do in this period? How to handle innovation?

Sometimes it is better to do nothing then to score own goals as this could be a turbulent time when it is better not to react. How to sense this or how to measure this state inside the company? Apart from numbers and all indicators, it is simply felt. The company is in a slowdown – maybe it is waiting for a merger or deep transformation and it is apparent that the quarterly results are not the best, there are no big investments, training courses have been cancelled and sometimes people are even laid off.

Dark times in corporations are simply times when there is no space or money for internal investments. This is a time when there is often no chance for innovation. One of the first persons in the company who will sense this is the innovation manager or chief innovation officer. She will first see the cutting in innovation budgets, and when the first slowdown results are presented to the employees the number of ideas submitted to innovation initiatives will rapidly decrease. In the worst case scenario, after layoffs, the innovation culture will be completely broken and it will have to be started from almost zero in the future when better times will come again for the company.

Most of the employees survive these turbulent times and continue to work as before. But innovation activities must be put aside for some time, as it would be counterproductive to ask innovators for ideas when there is no chance of having a budget or realising them.

So, how to run innovation activities in dark times? It is very difficult but not impossible. The biggest danger is to ruin future initiatives by starting something during a time when there's no chance of success. Innovation programmes or competitions during a bad time can put a "no chance" mark on an idea and this will make innovators unhappy and unmotivated for future initiatives. Also, some great ideas could be wrongly labelled and their destiny will be sealed.

Of course, not all activities should be stopped. Innovation groups could still communicate, trends and market insights must be gathered and improvements must be encouraged.

https://doi.org/10.1515/9783110654448-022

So as not to give all activities a rest in the time of slowdown, the focus could be turned to improvements. All process improvements and not-yet-known tools that save time (money) in some part of the company could be recognised and promoted. An example of this was shown in the chapter "Improvements in the Development Environment" (Example: innovation challenge for process improvements).

What can an innovator or innovation practitioner do in these times?

Take your hands off innovation activities for a period of time, prepare for a new reset and how things will go from there. So, be prepared and wait ... But, do not wait too long, if the times aren't getting better maybe it's your turn to make them so. Surely, this is the time for self-education and preparing for the next challenges.

When is the right time to get out of the shadow and present your ideas? When is it time to step up with something new and shiny after a time of darkness?

With the first rays of sunshine, innovation can be started as it flourishes best in a time of growth when it has all the necessary support. After every period of turmoil, a business gets "reset". Often, the best messenger of better times to employees is a new innovation programme or initiative.

A welcome option may be to make innovation part of redefining the company (in the event that the company is going downwards). In that case, innovation activities should be adapted and highlighted as a priority. This will surely get attention, but also put more weight on the shoulders of the person responsible for innovation; during that time, innovation measures, which should give the company a new start, will be difficult to execute. Of course, without clear support from all stakeholders and employees, these efforts could be counterproductive.

On the other hand, the crisis can create a symbiosis between management, sales, product line and experts and lead to new ideas that will result in necessary changes and maybe also changes – pivot – in strategy. This is a time when education plays a big role, not only for experts and innovators, but also for executives who must be aware of all disturbances that are occurring in order to be able to act. If there is a need to come to new ideas, in these times the first persons to be counted on are members of the innovators group and the previous efforts of establishing such group can now be praised. To summarise, innovation could be a part of crisis management, but this must be done very carefully.

Example: Case of failure

A software company which started declining in all figures, decided to narrow their portfolio and focus on three sectors. Among those three sectors, they decided to add most investments to the smallest (not yet developed) sector, the one where they had the least knowledge. The top-down idea was ignited when one executive had a hunch about trends in that sector and the company listened and placed nearly all their hope on that department and innovator.

The start wasn't good, it wasn't easy to find developers and managers, and many people from many locations were brought together to make the still unclear product. Do I need to say that the project was managed chaotically? After several months, they had a prototype, and after many attempts, conferences and sales pitches they got their first customer.

The deal wasn't good, but they could learn from it and it would make things a bit easier to defend at the next executive meeting. During that time, all other departments that were prosperous couldn't afford growth as most of the profit was going to this sector. They were in a trap, as they already thought that it was now too late to stop as too many resources had already been spent. So, all eyes were watching the first customer, but the product was still not good enough and all efforts were useless. In the end, the company closed this business that generated only losses without a second customer.

The key here was to know when to stop. The lesson learned was to try not to invest in the wrong direction, but even if it happens (and it must be done sometimes) it is essential not to be stubborn when everything is telling you to stop. Even big companies can fall into this trap – imagine, then, how easy it is for small ones or startups to get into this position.

Example: Death of the long-lasting product

I was working on a long-lasting product which was generating project after project for customers all over the world over a period of 10 years. The product was reaching its peak and everyone was aware of it, from product managers to developers. Something needed to be done and the budget was allocated for a totally new version of the product that had to be developed from scratch. The best developers were transferred to the project and they worked on it for months, but in the end, after spending much time and resources, everything was abandoned as the market turned to other, cheaper products that had showed up in the meantime. The competition used newer technologies and was quicker and more adaptable in responding to the needs of the customer. In a matter of a few months, all project members were moved to other products and this product just died.

This is an example of a product were innovation was done at the right time, but the market still turned to another product.

23 Technology Management

> Product management really is the fusion between technology, what engineers do – and the
> business side. — Marissa Mayer

After many chapters about innovation management, let's say a few words about the closest and overlapping topic. In some companies, these are also tied together as innovation and technology management.

What is technology management? For all organisations in today's world, it is necessary to concentrate on driving products and processes with implementation planning and organisation, evaluation of trends, market objectives, future scenarios, strategic planning and training of the workforce.

It is defined as a set of management disciplines that allows organisations to manage their technological fundamentals to create a competitive advantage. It is supported by these six pillars (shown in Figure 23.1):

- Trends: forecasting possible relevant technologies in the present and near future. Also, look for possible new directions where the market is heading.
- Events: internal forums, conferences and other events that will tie together all company experts and foster communication between them. Events could be created around a special topic that will widen everyone's perspective and make this topic acknowledged inside the company.
- Supporting innovation process: these two disciplines are closely connected and must be intertwined.
- Cooperation: establishing external connections could be essential to the prosperity of the organisation.
- Roadmap: mapping technologies to market and business perspectives and aligning them to the strategy of the organisation. Also, keep all resources and build a kind of repository where all company knowledge is marked. Archive past projects and products so that there will be no chance of doing the same thing twice (especially necessary for bigger companies).
- Education: make a proposal for workforce education in the short term and long term.

Additionally, connections with customers should be established in order to get market insights – first, by closely connecting with product managers and then by establishing a connection with salespeople.

A recent study[85] found that *sensing and finding new technology trends* is the most important internal process or asset for successful innovation in companies. The second

---

85 Deloitte Insights: Innovation in Europe, A Deloitte survey on European companies and how digital technologies can strategically enhance innovation, 2019 Deloitte Development LLC.

https://doi.org/10.1515/9783110654448-023

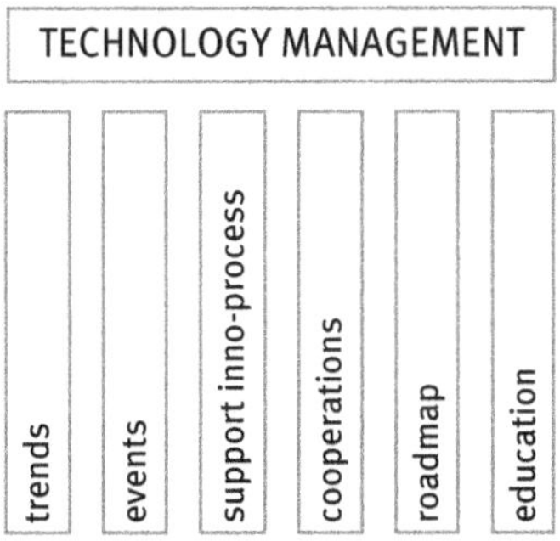

TECHNOLOGY MANAGEMENT

trends | events | support inno-process | cooperations | roadmap | education

Figure 23.1: Technology management.

most important process or asset is *innovation strategy design and setting aspirations*. By way of contrast, the main obstacle to fostering innovation in a company are *sensing and scanning technology trends* (first) and *lack of technology skills* (third).

Every new technology, before it's used in a company, first needs to be understood. Its value and prosperity may be identified through a network of experts formed by technology management. Then those technologies can be further monitored, introduced, researched and developed inside the organisation. Sometimes technologies don't fit the company strategy or portfolio and they must be dropped;, this is also one of technology management's tasks.

Technology management should help the company be attractive by adding the possibility of identifying new technologies and implementing them. It also shows how the company can be proactive on the market and not wait for others, marking itself as a "follower".

A key role is played by the technology manager, who must obtain and digest all information, use a network of technology experts for evaluation of trends. and shape any necessary information for global communication. The technology manager does not make strategy decisions, as her role is to prepare the ground for them.

At the start, the company must be scanned for experts as they could provide an opinion about the current and future strategy of the company. Influential experts could spread a new climate among their colleagues. Later, the network of experts must be carefully built, managed and constantly expanded using the support of human resources and innovation management. Use of this network should allow the possibility of further expression – through blogs or corporate articles – a way in which experts could share their findings and thoughts in the company.

Experts group

An expert is a man who has made all the mistakes that can be made, in a narrow field.
– Niels Bohr

Experts can be grouped into a special entity, which could gather, discuss and propose new trends and technologies.

An example of an experts group comes from Atos, a global leader in digital transformation with over 110,000 employees in 73 countries who are developing and implementing innovative digital solutions.[86] Their expert community has over 2,000 members across the globe, specialising in a range of subjects from infrastructure to quantum to digital workplaces and everything in between. Their experts have the freedom and support from the business to continue to learn, discuss and experiment. Additionally, an Expert Community Convention is held every year to foster technical collaboration, ideation and interaction with Atos experts, partners and startups, as well as to share the group's future technology directions.

Forums

One particularly loved method inside software development communities (companies) is a forum. This is a regularly scheduled talk about a proposed topic where invited guests talk in a relaxed atmosphere. The topic could be presented at the start, but the forum can also go on without a presentation. An example is where some new technology or process is introduced and then a series of forums are scheduled to evangelize the crowd. This method could be quite effective and it could help in changing the thinking inside the environment. In the past, exactly this kind of method was used in some companies to spread agile thinking and methodology.

---

86 https://atos.net/en/.

24 The Effect

No organization ever created an innovation. People innovate, not companies.   – Seth Godin

We created an innovation initiative, supported technology management activities, but when do we know that we succeeded? An innovation system should help companies in implementing an innovation strategy and generate results. The process must be constantly adapted with proven techniques to improve innovation management performance.

First, there are different expectations from different stakeholders. Executives expect the growth of their company. Salespeople have targets, which means the same – growth. Product managers target new products or improved new versions of old products. The next group – delivery teams – want to have a successful development process with people who are satisfied and (if possible) loyal.

Figure 24.1 shows the graphical representation of the effect that innovation activities should have on software companies.

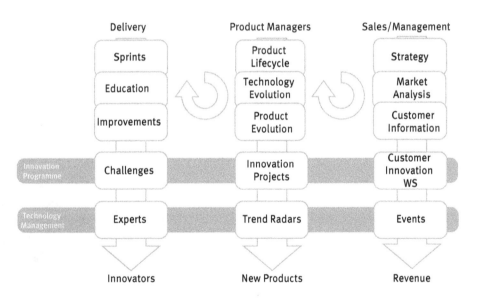

Figure 24.1: The effect.

The delivery process (as shown in the picture) is running in sprint after sprint in its circles. Education and continuous improvements should be part of this process, even though they are sometimes put aside.

https://doi.org/10.1515/9783110654448-024

The product management process is done inside the product lifecycle. It must look outside for new technologies and possible product evolutions (forced by the market).

Executives and salespeople are using market analysis and customer information to help other pillars of this system using the company strategy.

All three pillars are tightly connected and one of the strongest connections should be the innovation programme, which has initiatives that every stakeholder should support. Innovation challenges should create innovators out of "ordinary" developers or managers. This should result in innovation projects, which should add value primarily to product managers. One of the targets – customer innovation workshops – should be held by connecting customers, innovation managers, innovators, product managers, salespeople and executives.

In the end, technology management should make further connections by linking experts in the company and using technology and trend radars and events to promote new trends and technologies all over the organisation.

Together these methods should create or upgrade an innovation system which should discover and nurture innovators, add value and prolong the successful life of the company.

Further Reading

I would like to recommend some books, as these books changed the way I think about this topic. I also included some quotes or thoughts from these books. Here is the list:

Brad Murphy, Dr. Carol Mase: The Age of Surge: A Human Centered Framework for Scaling Company-Wide Agility and Navigating the Tsunami of Digital

Max Mckeown: The Innovation Book: How to manage ideas and execution for outstanding results

Davila, Epstein: Making Innovation Work: How to Manage It, Measure It, and Profit from It

Davila, Epstein: The Innovation Paradox, Why Good Businesses Kill Breakthroughs and How They Can Change

Langdon Morris: The Agile Innovation

Tom Kelley: The Ten Faces of Innovation: Ideo's Strategies for Beating the Devil's Advocate and Driving Creativity Throughout Your Organization

Tom and David Kelley: Creative Confidence: Unleashing the Creative Potential within Us All

Jeffrey Phillips: Relentless Innovation: What Works, What Doesn't – And What That Means For Your Business

Jake Knapp, John Zeratsky, Braden Kowitz: Sprint: How to Solve Big Problems and Test New Ideas in Just Five Days

https://doi.org/10.1515/9783110654448-025

About

Tomislav Buljubašić has more than a decade of experience in raising innovation culture, scouting new technology trends and creating innovation programmes and campaigns. He created an innovation reward programme and a series of inno-challenges tailored for software developers. Through many trainings, he promotes ways of thinking using future scenarios and builds a capacity to innovate. He authored "Free your Creativity", a manual for starters and "Creative Cards", an innovation-stimulating tool.

Find more material about his work on 7innovation.net. Join the conversation about innovation and creativity by following him on Twitter @buljubasict

Based in Croatia, he works at the IT Company Enea Software. He is a proud member and supporter of NK Osijek.

https://doi.org/10.1515/9783110654448-026

Thanks

A big thanks goes to my wife, Dragana, who provided me with litres of lemonade, and to my sons, Jan and Darin. They were patient and full of support while I was writing this book. Thanks to my parents, Nevenka and Ivica, who opened the world for me and my sister Marija.

People who helped me in reviewing: Denis Faivre, Blaž Vincetić and Stanislav Strešnjak.

People who helped me bringing their cases studies: Carina Leue-Bensch (Lufthansa Systems), Hrvoje Hadžić (Ericsson Nikola Tesla), Alex Goryachev (Cisco), Susana Jurado Apruzzese (Telefonica) and Denis Faivre (Worldline).

Additional thanks to Hans-Juergen August, Michael Jagersberger and Oliver Korfmacher.

https://doi.org/10.1515/9783110654448-027

Index

https://doi.org/10.1515/9783110654448-028